Fantasy Doodles

by Roan Tjon-fo

FB@Fantasy Doodles By Roan
IG@Rootje23

Copyright © 2017
No part of this book my be reproduced in any form by print, photocopy, or any other means without prior written permission from the publisher.

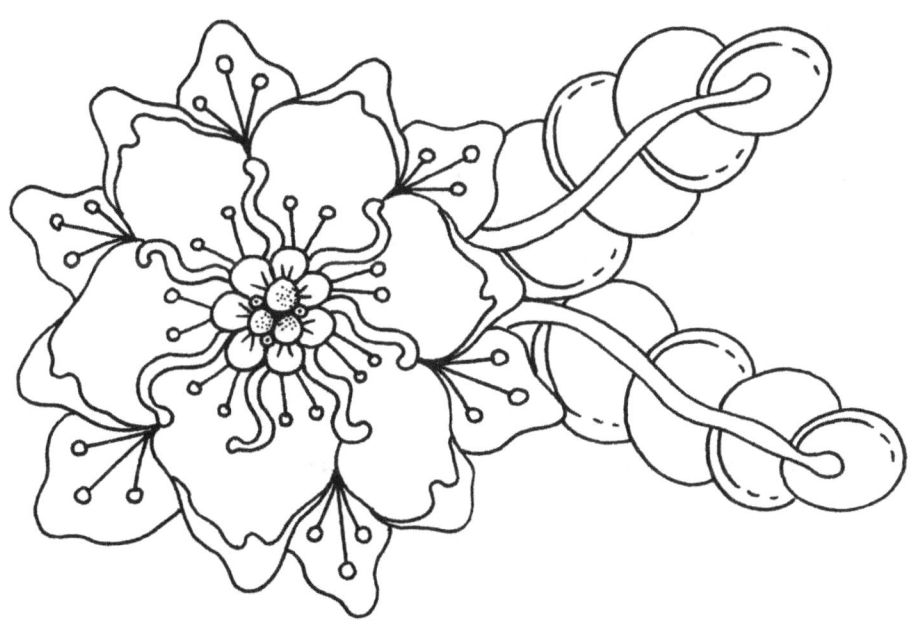

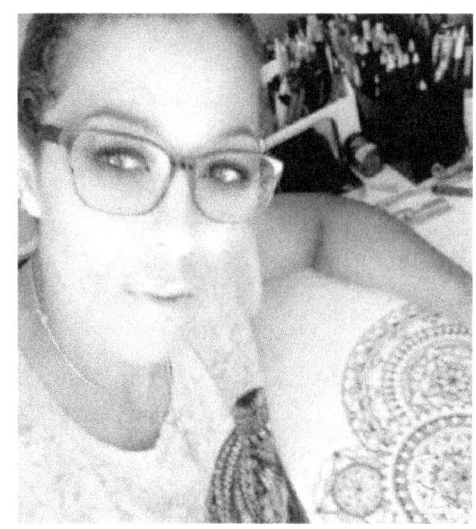

Hi! Let me introduce myself..

My name is Roan Tjon-Fo, a self-taught doodle artist from the Netherlands, a creative person with way too many passions.

A few years ago i decided to focus on drawing only, because it calms me. It's very relaxing for me to put my pen on some paper and just wait and see what flows out of my hand, the most ideas come as they are, i don't have a set pattern in my head beforehand.

I wish you all a lot of fun with coloring in the various designs, and hope that it works just as relaxing for you, as it was for me while creating them.

I would love to see your coloring creations, you can always tag me on

Instagram @Rootje23

Facebook @Fantasy doodles by Roan

My first color book Fantasy Feathers 2016

My second color book Fantasy Doodles 2017

Tips:

Markers or gel pen: Don't press too hard so that the paper doesn't swell up.

Use a piece of cardboard under the drawing paper so that it doesn't bleed through to the paper underneath.

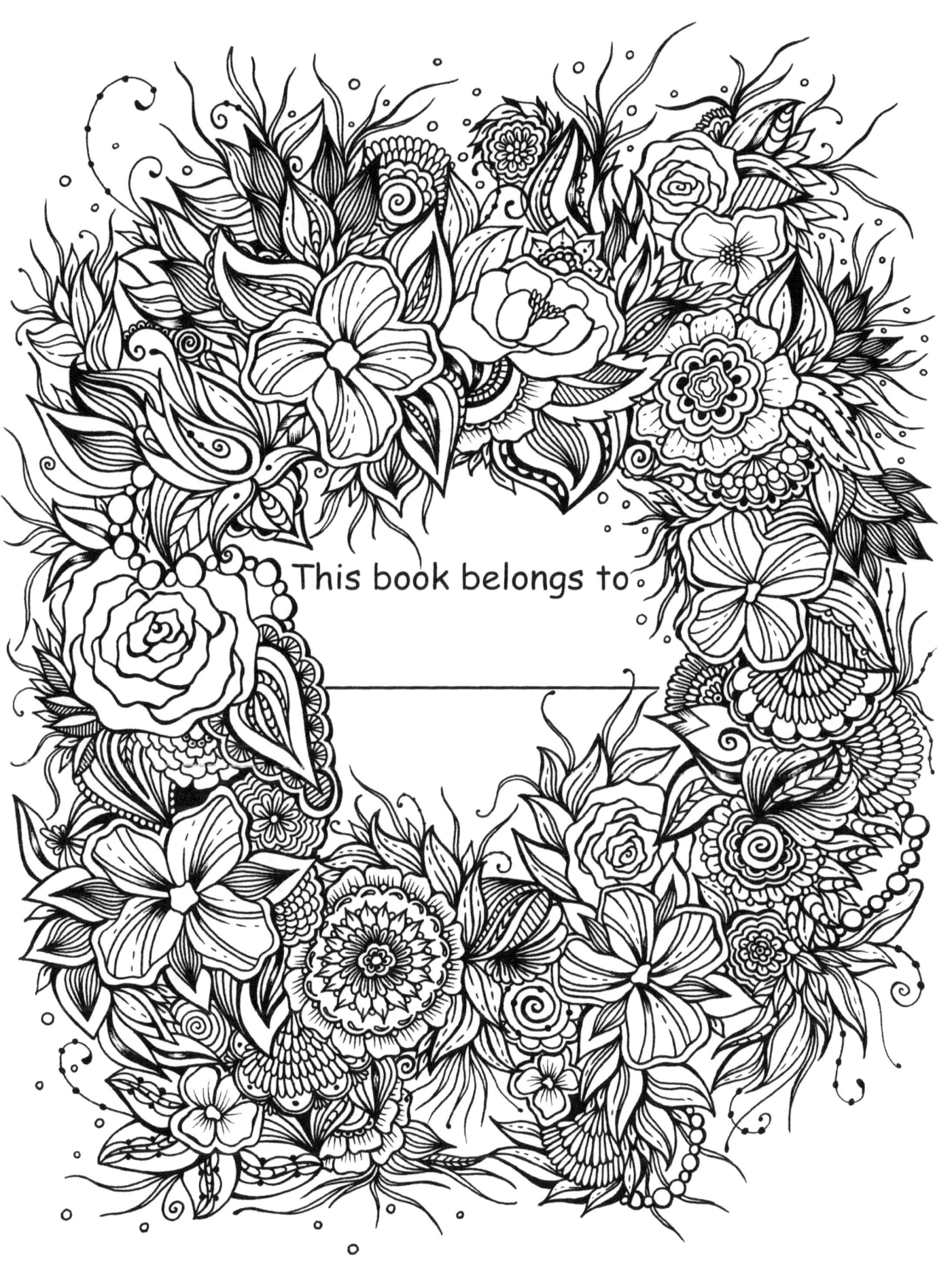

This book belongs to
_____

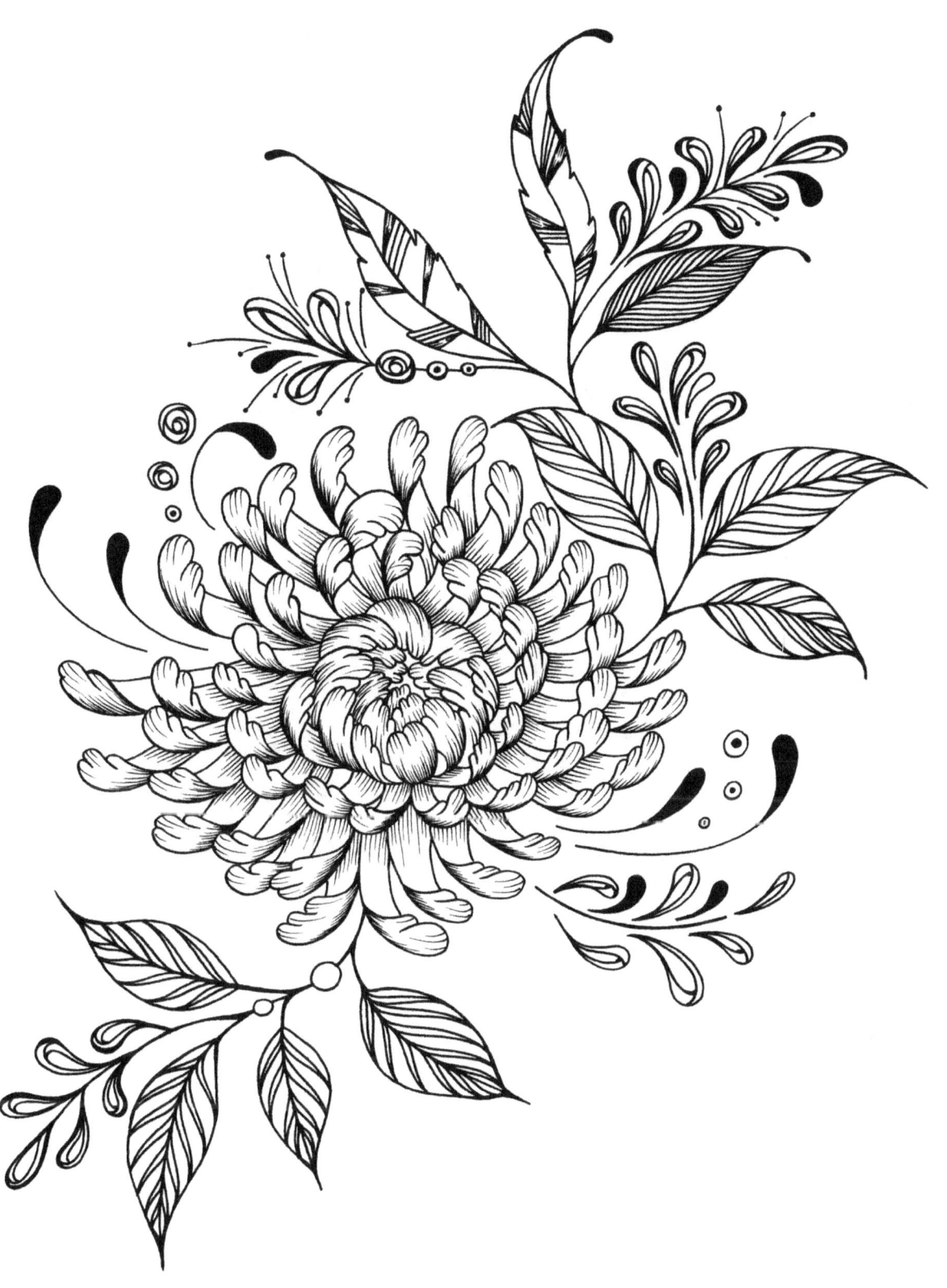

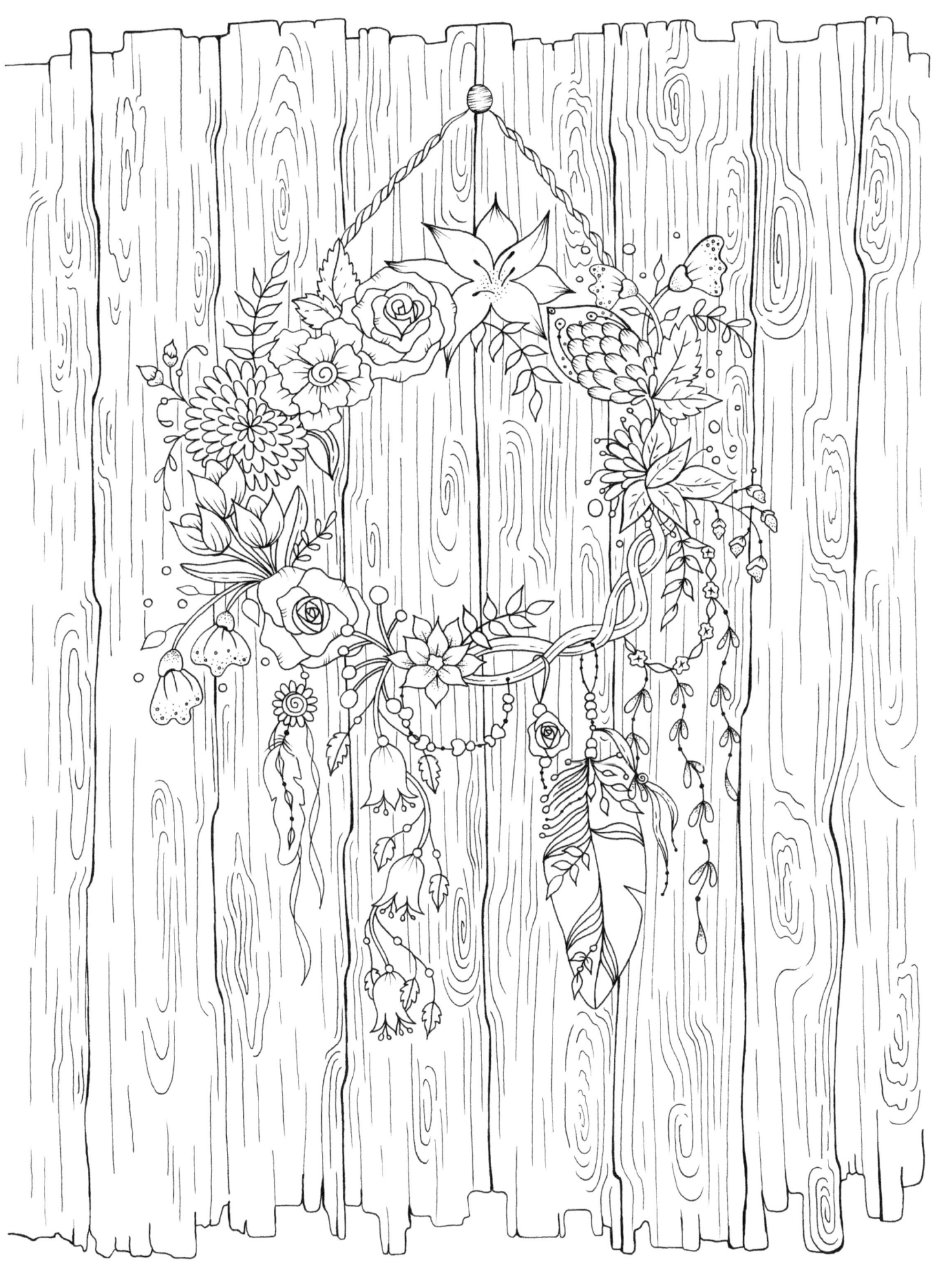

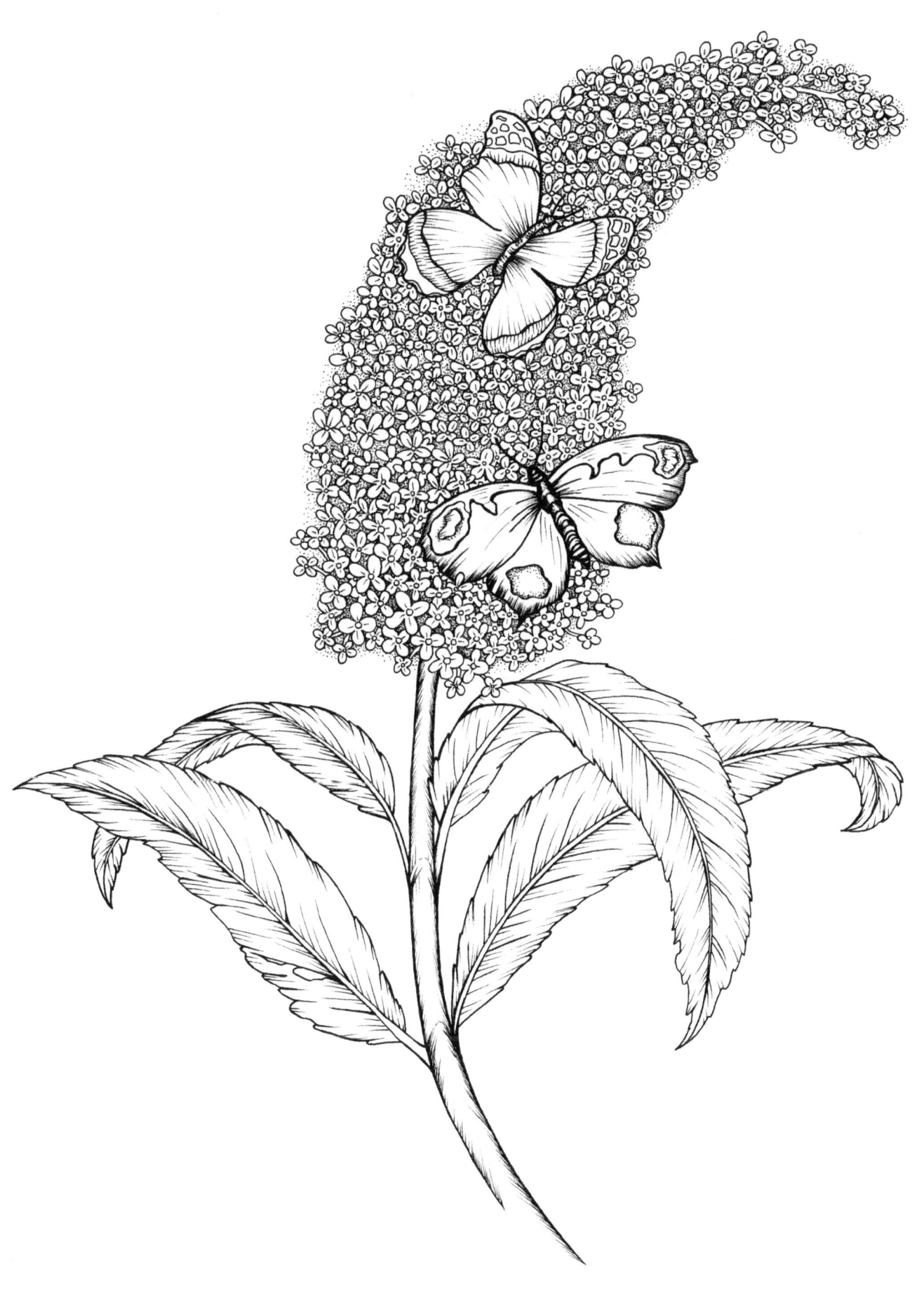

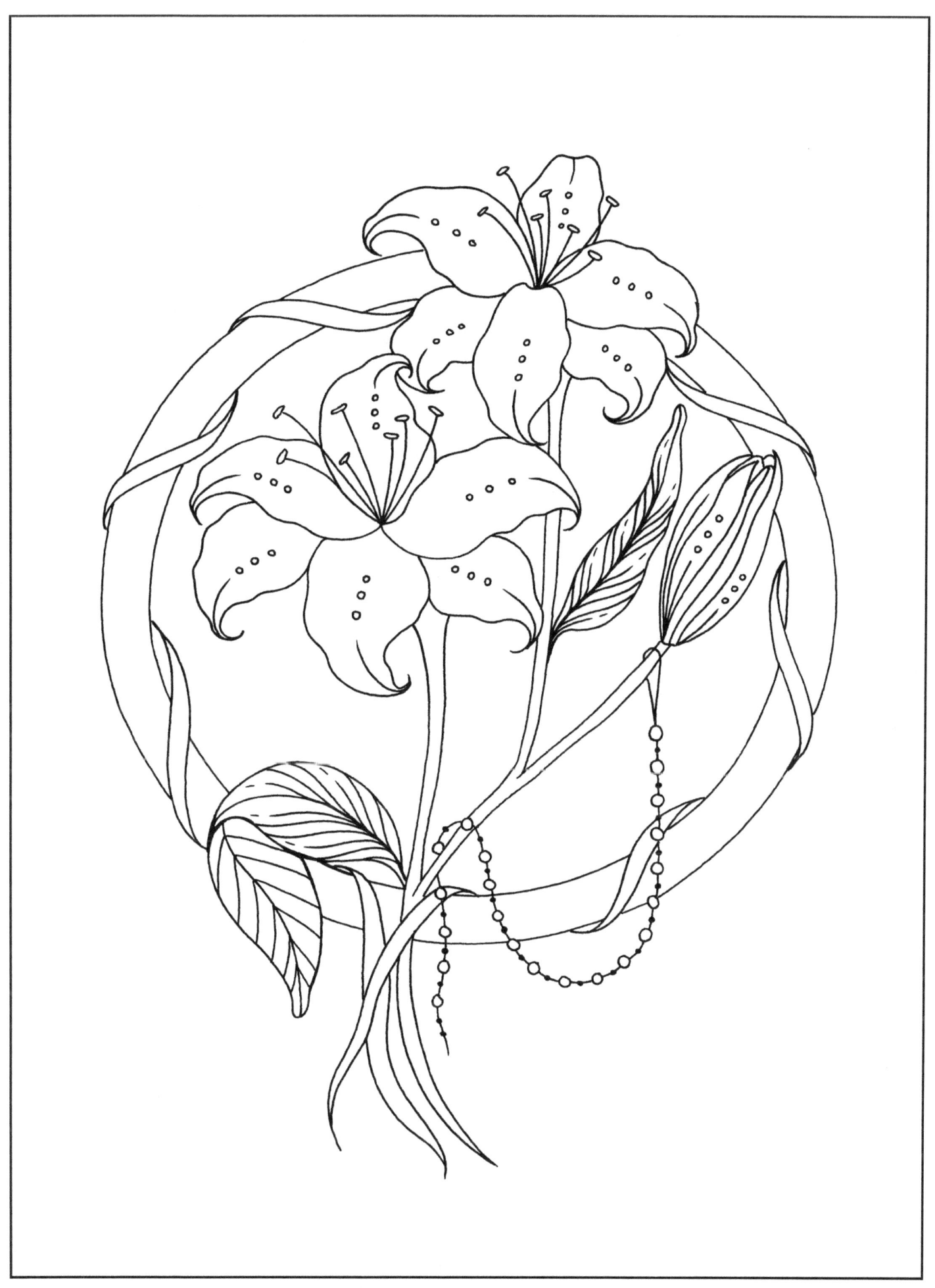

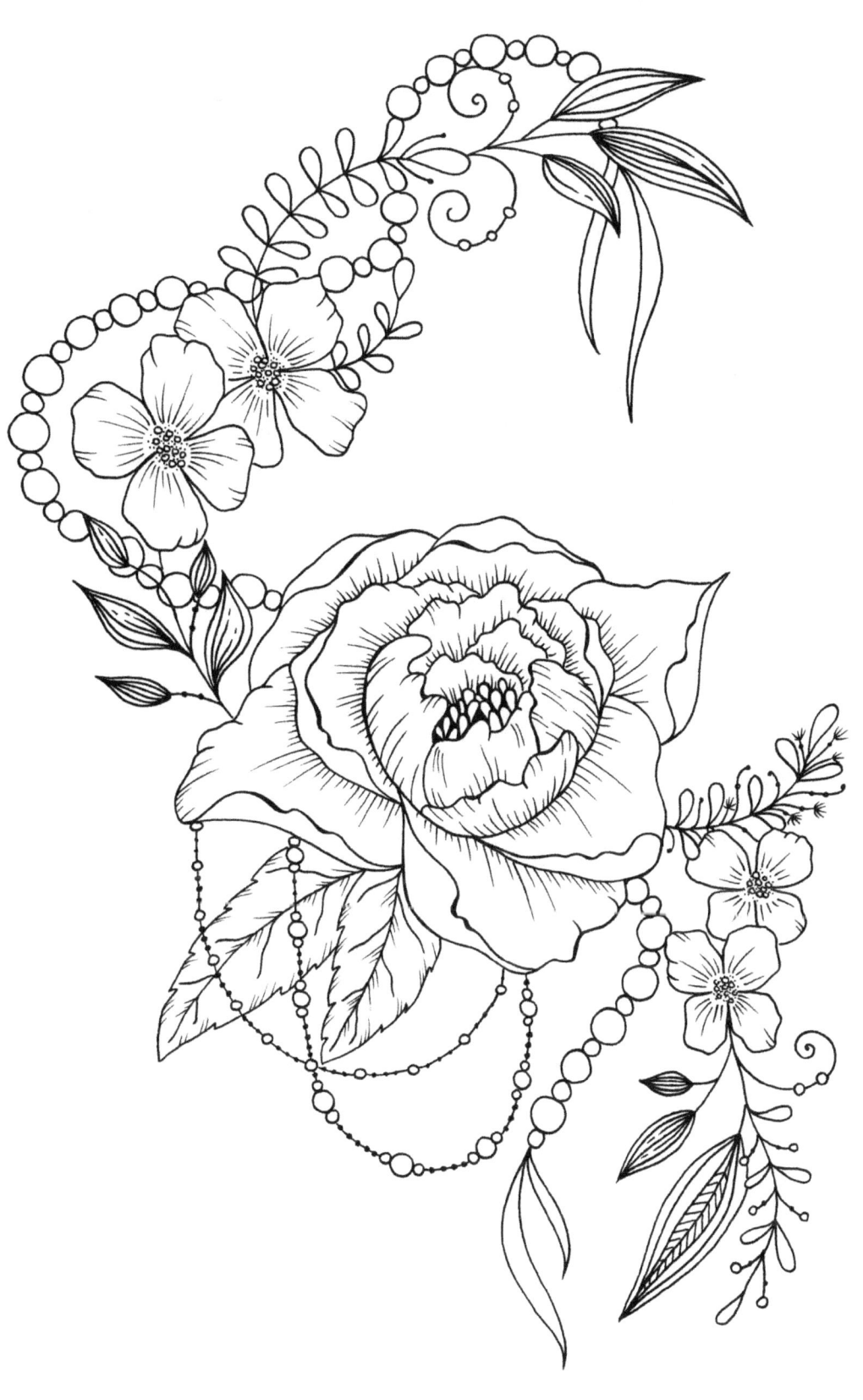

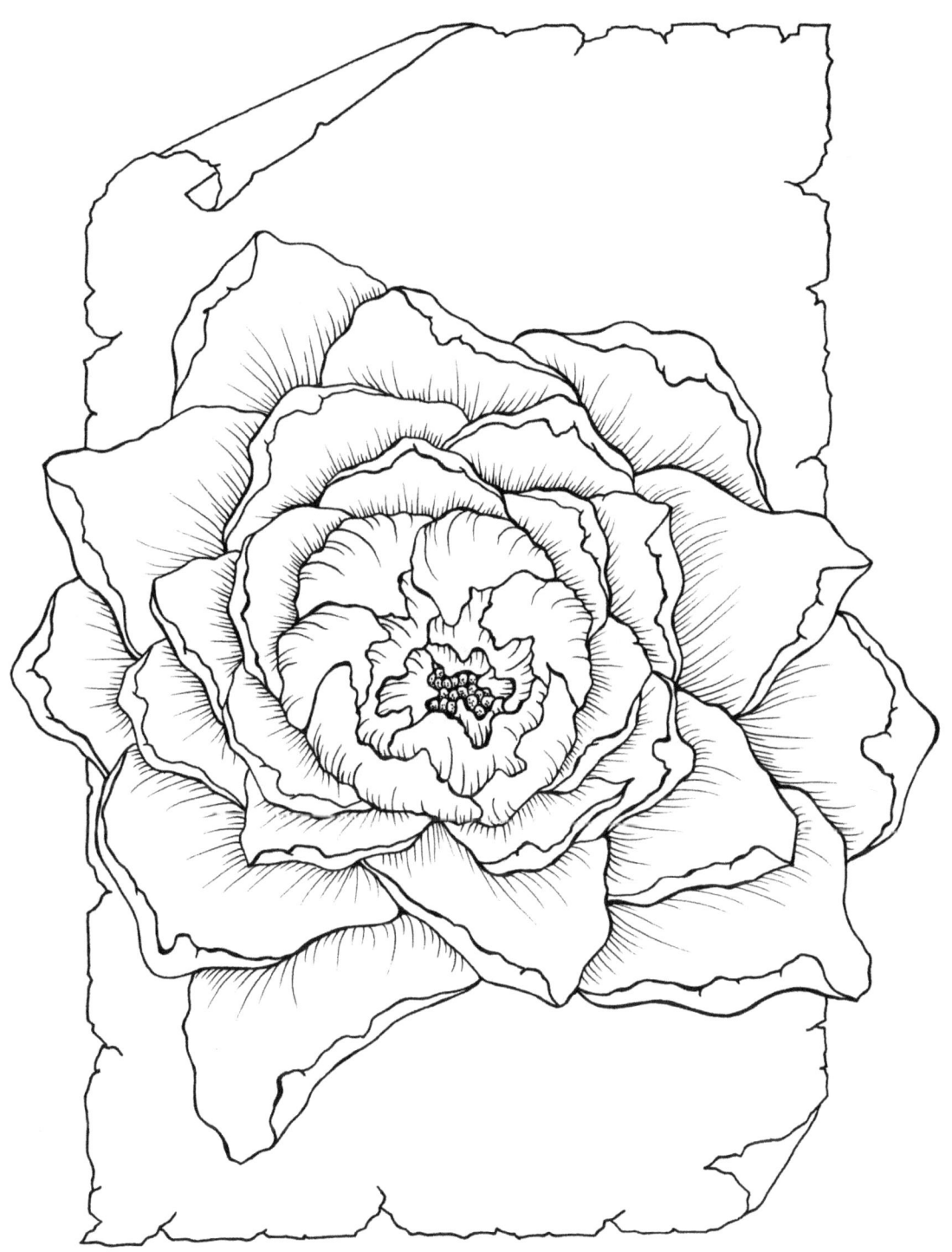

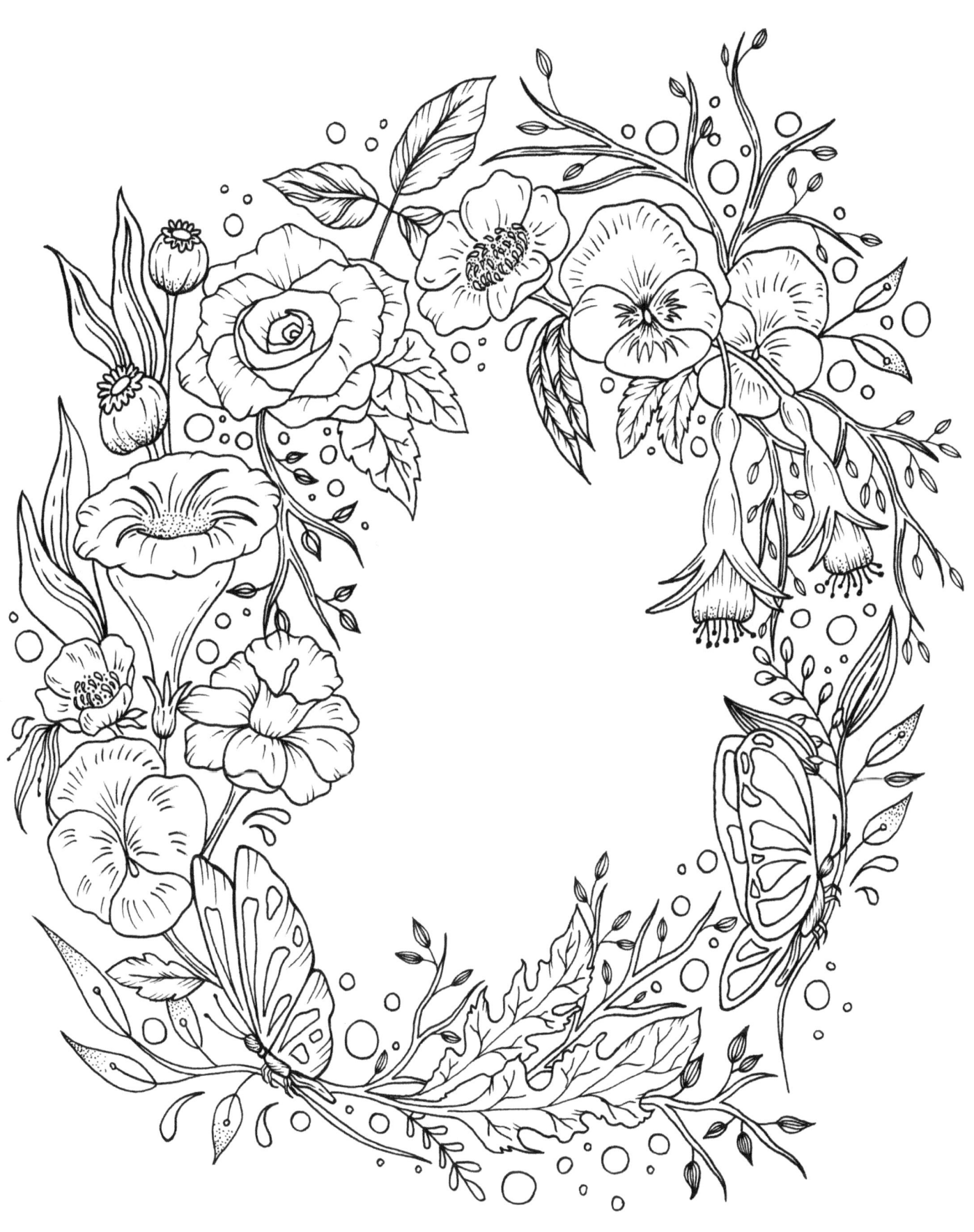

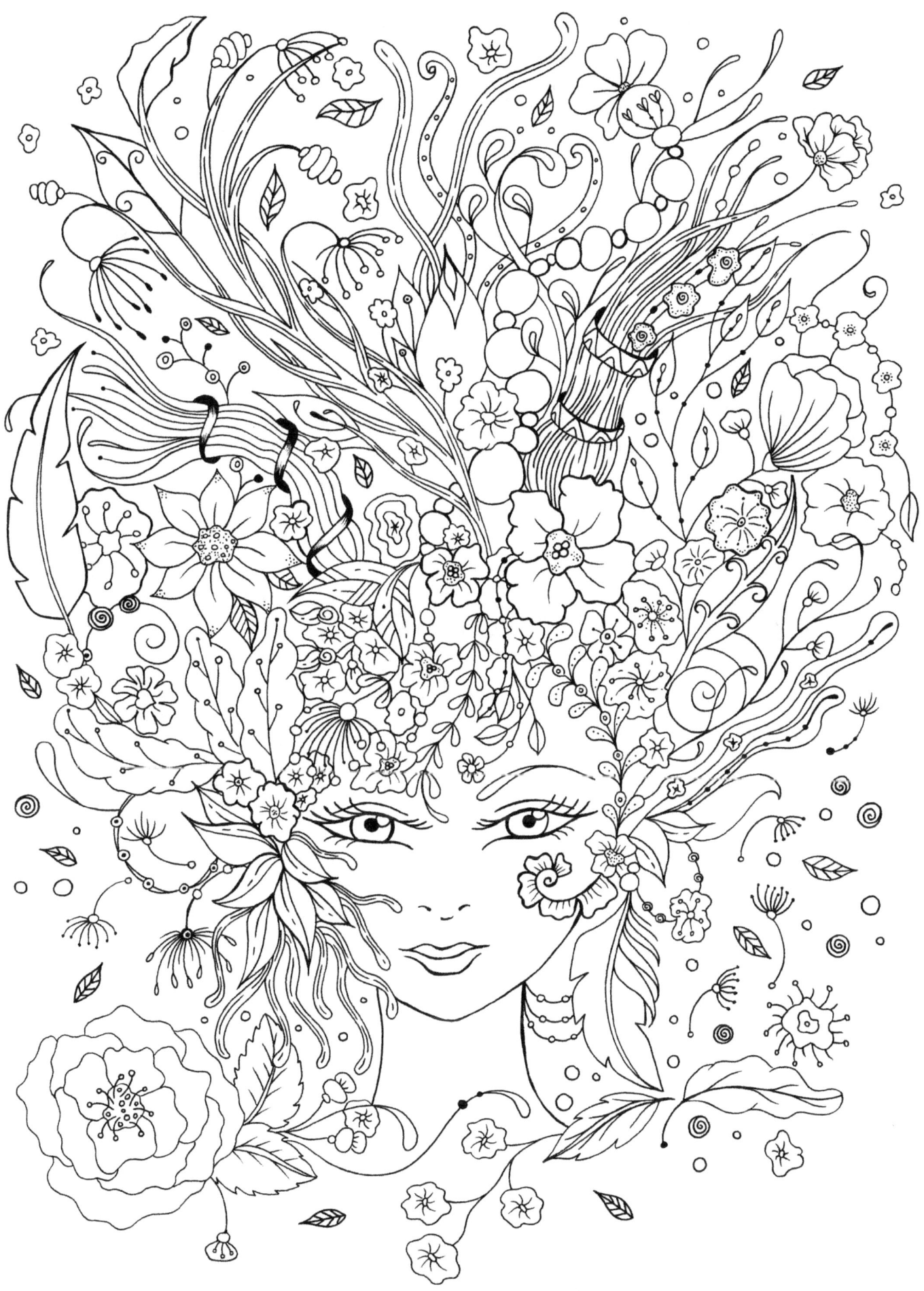

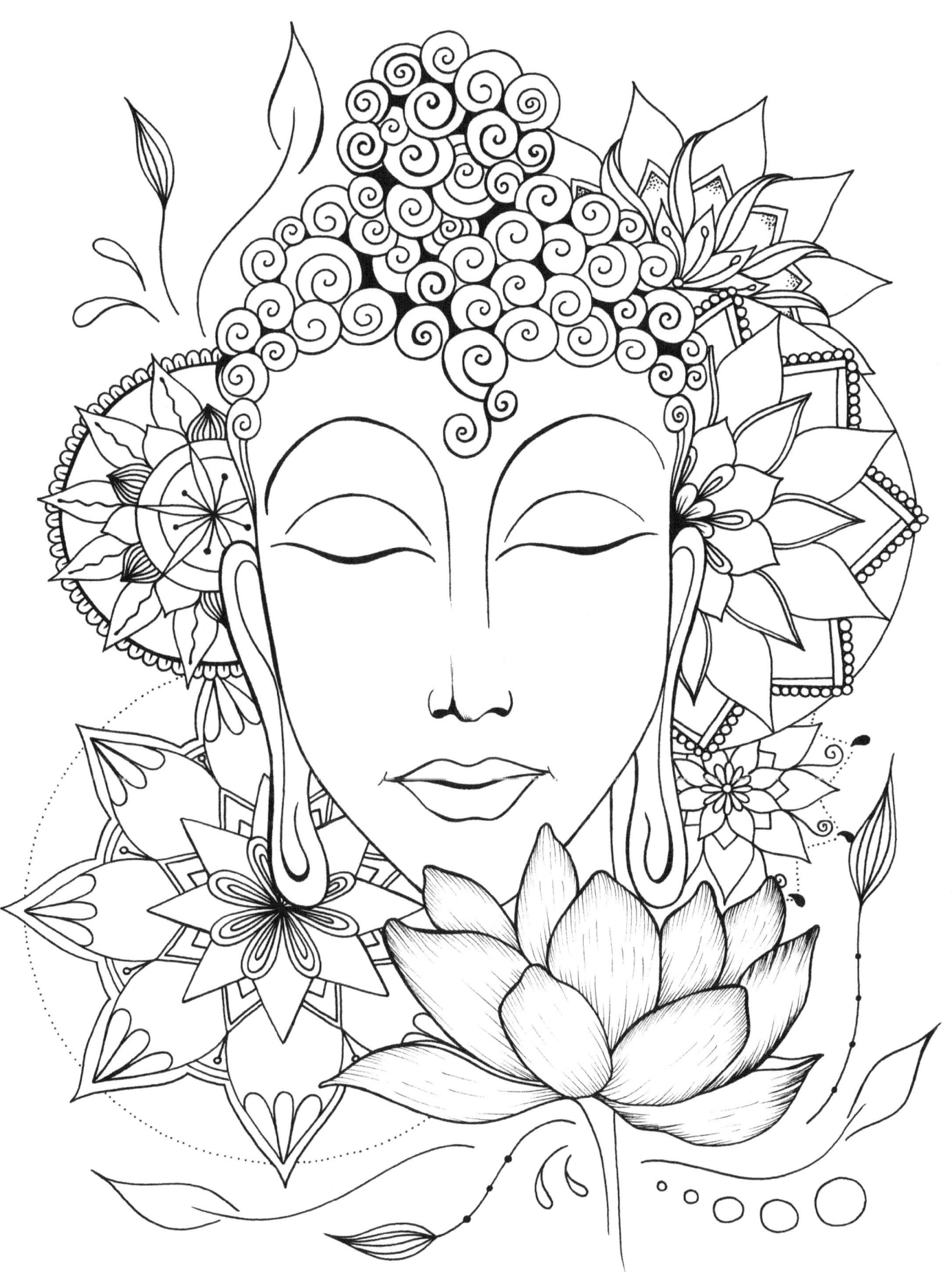

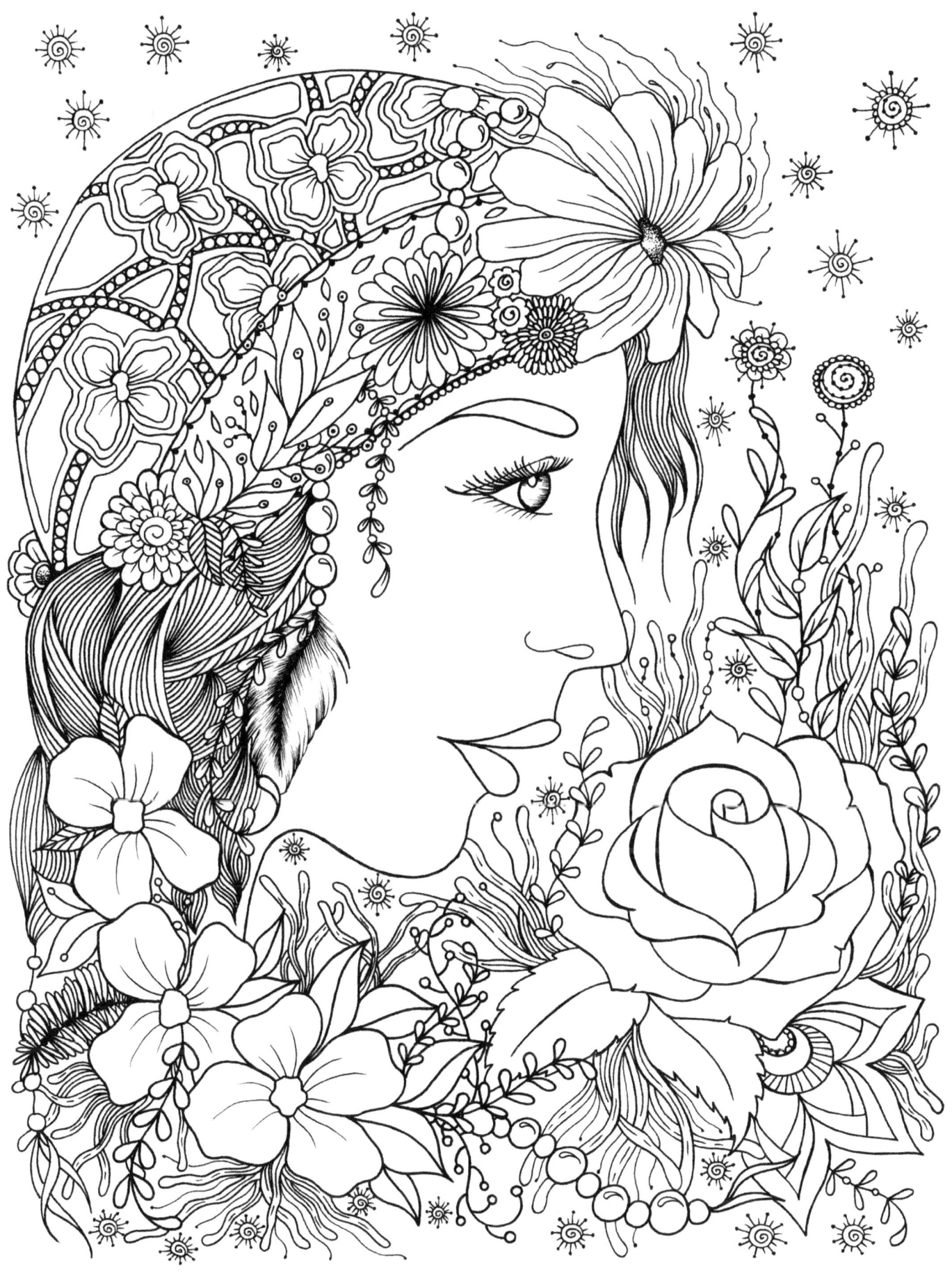

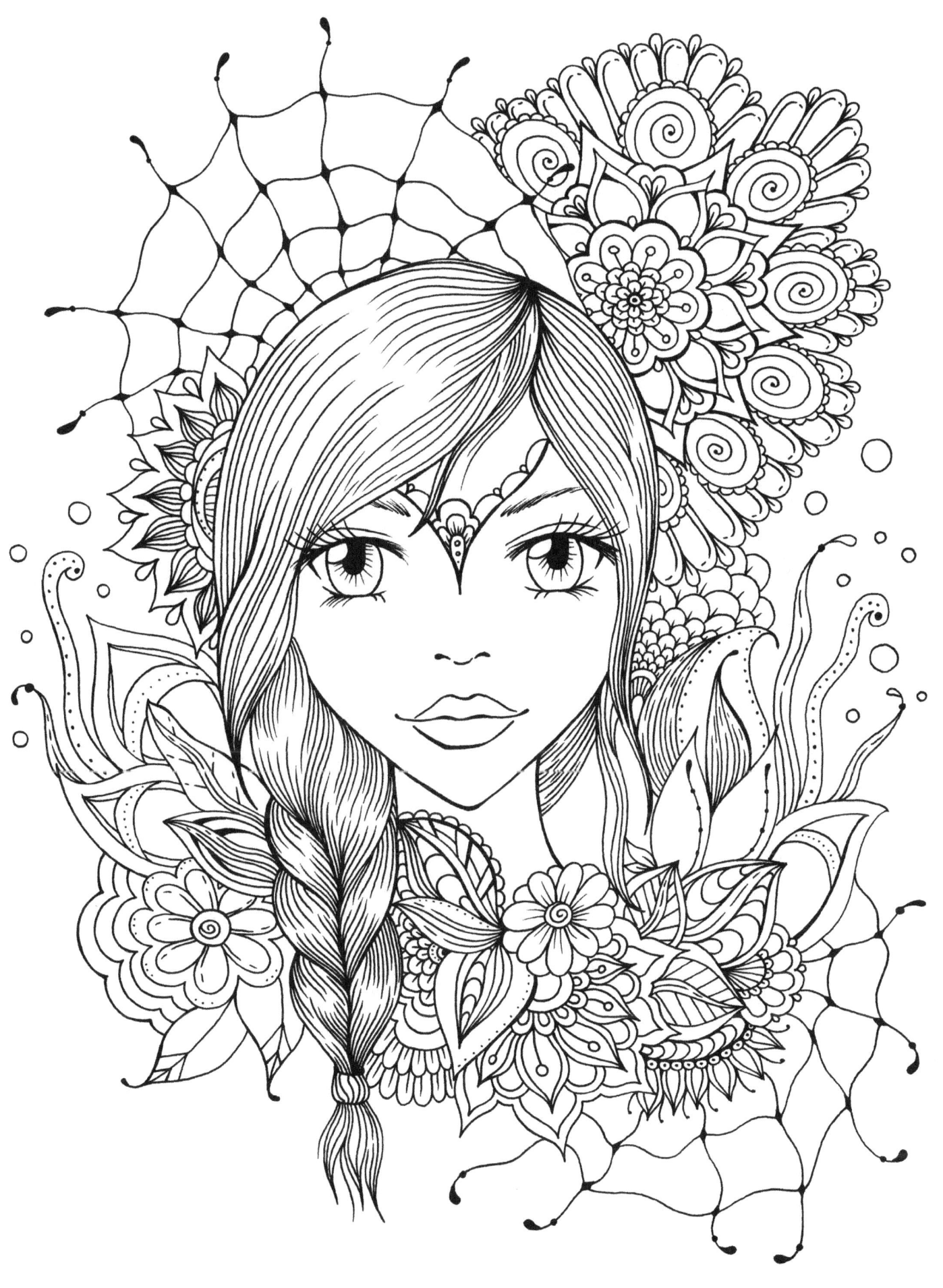

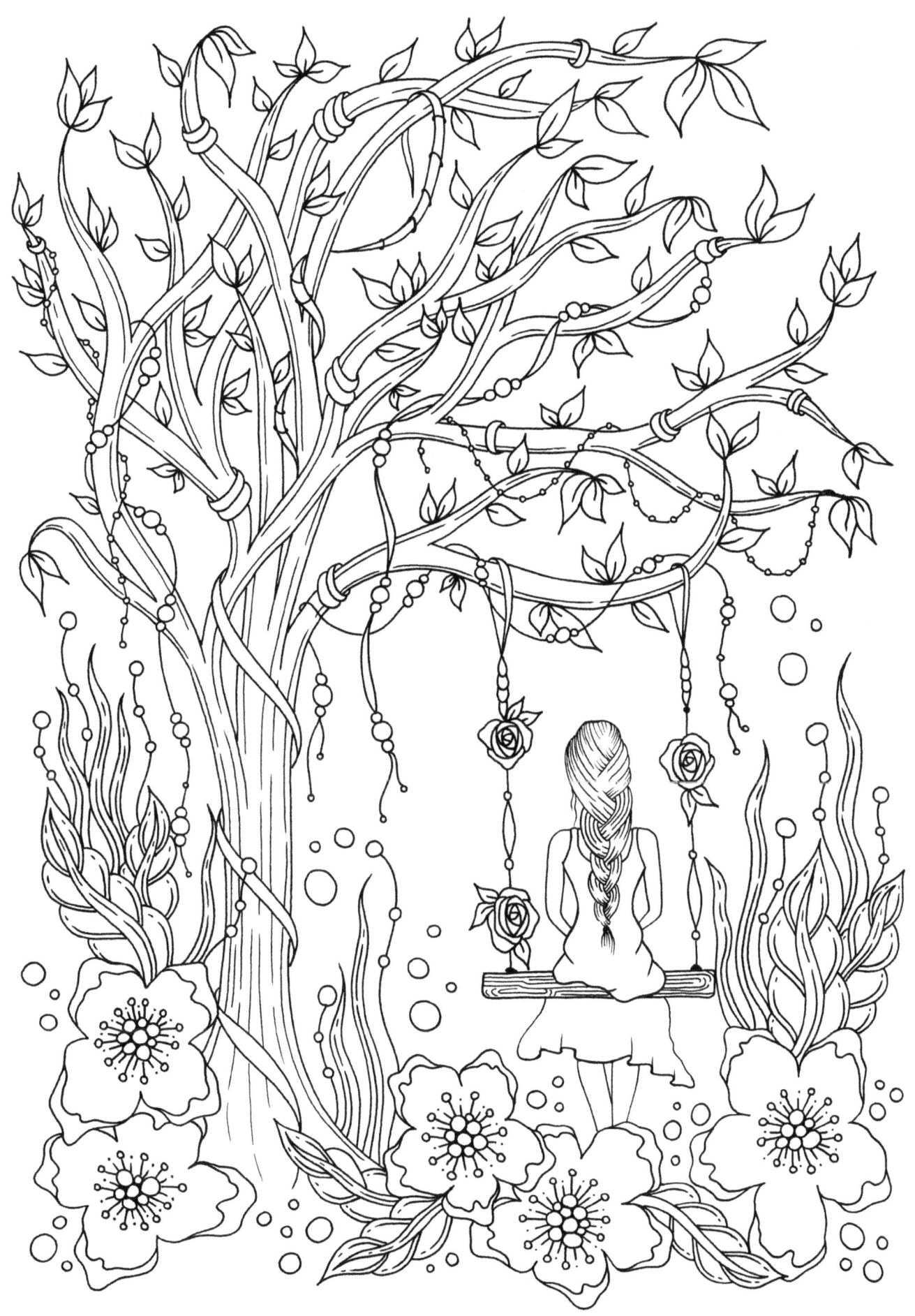

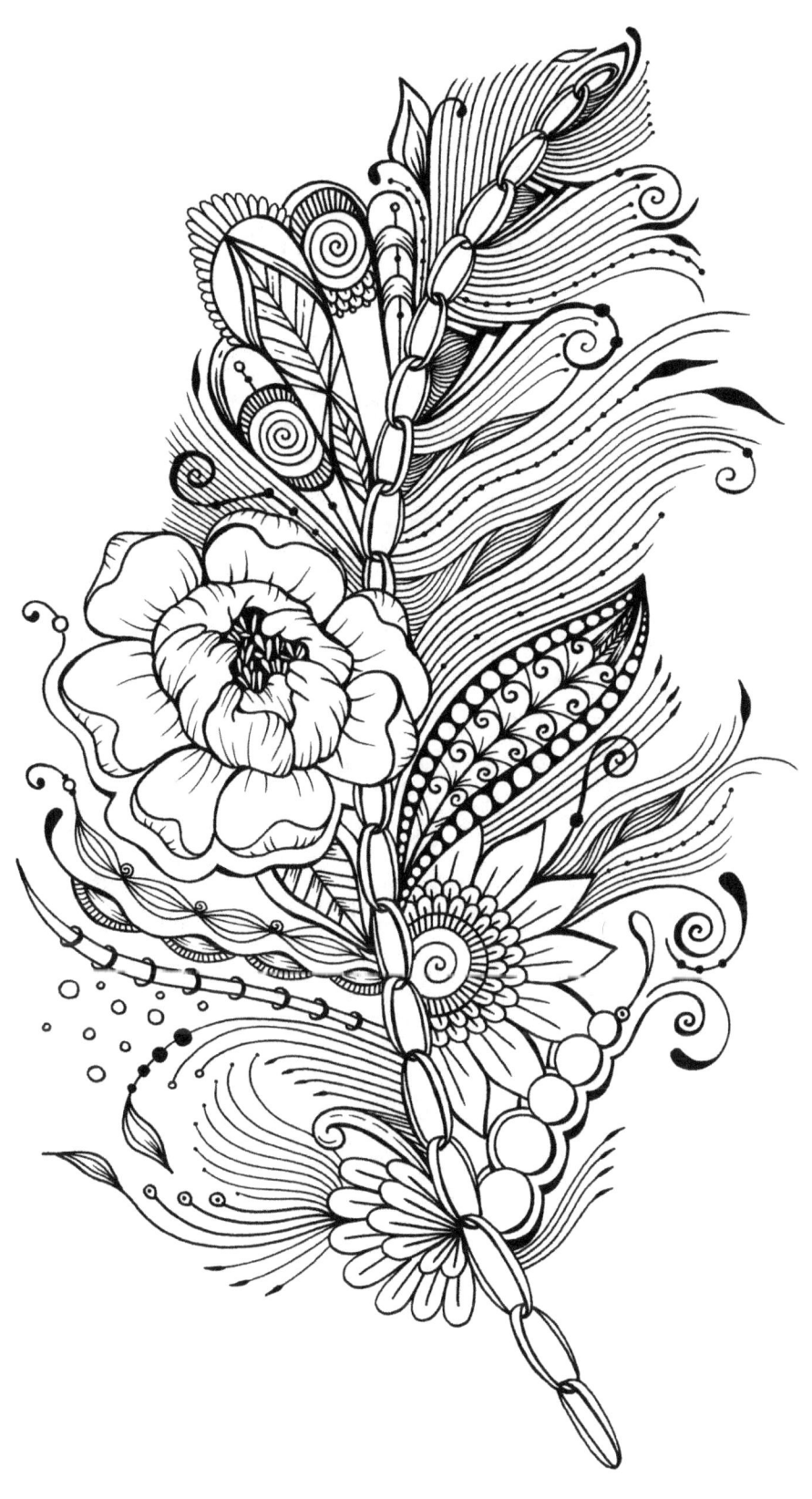

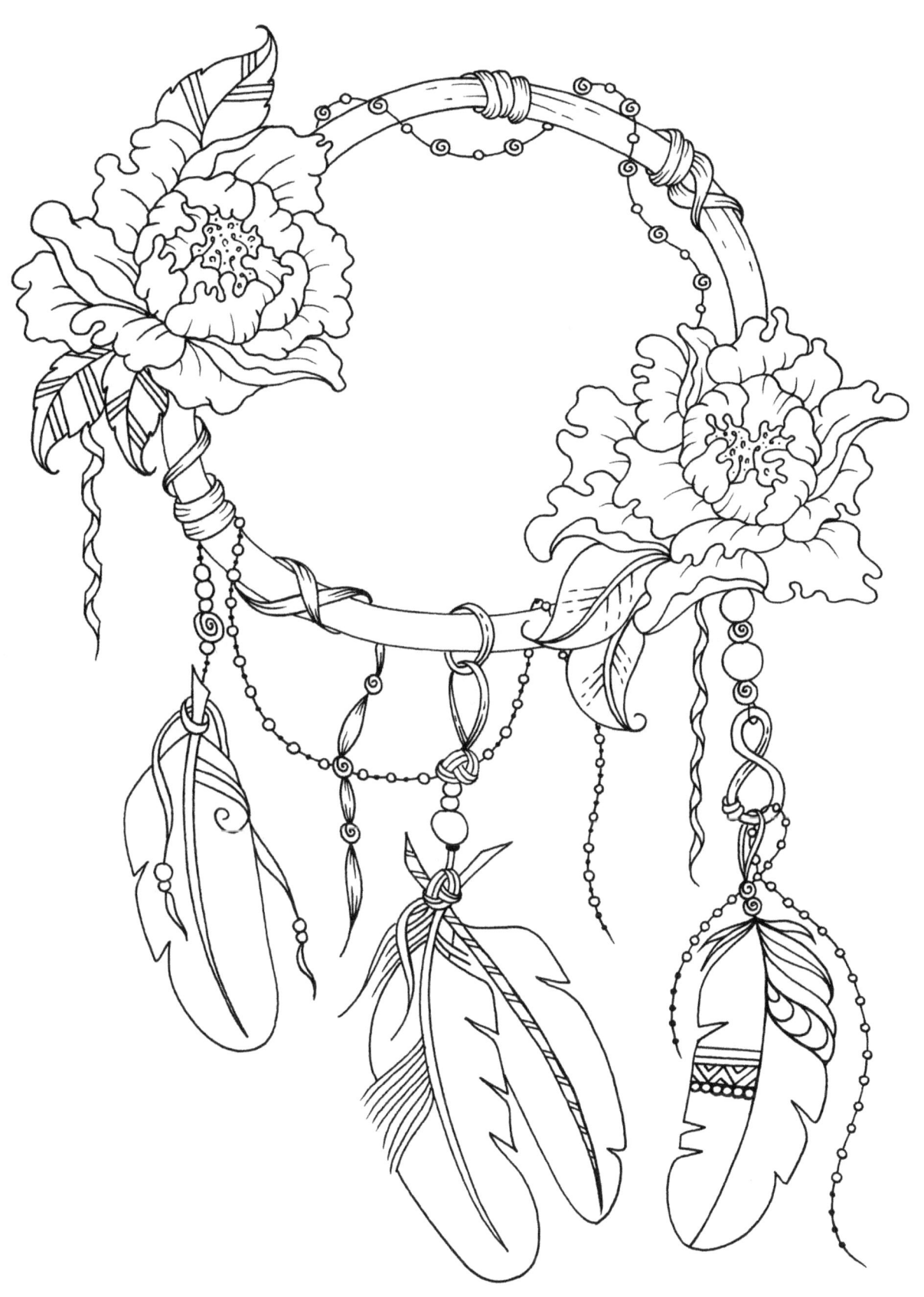

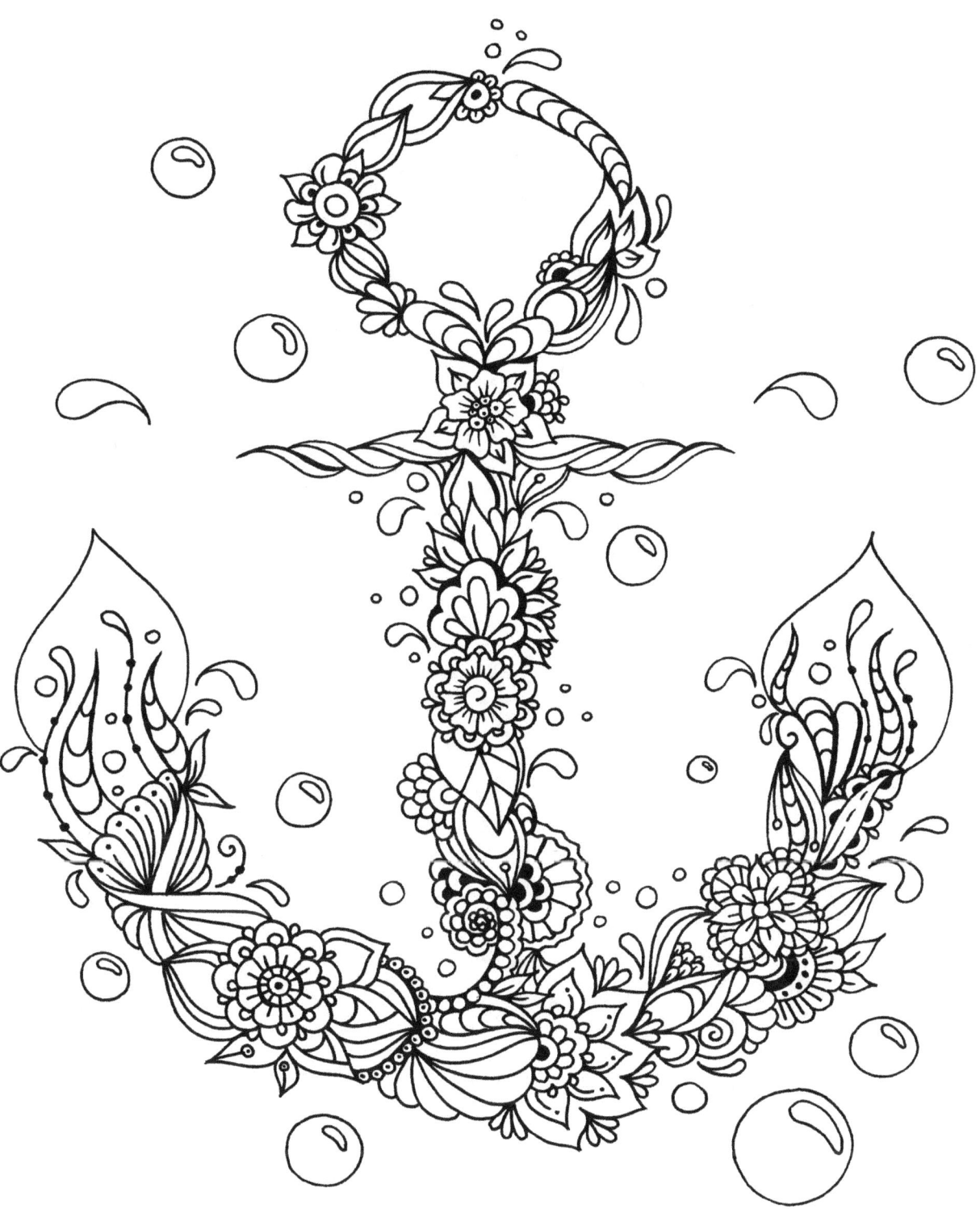

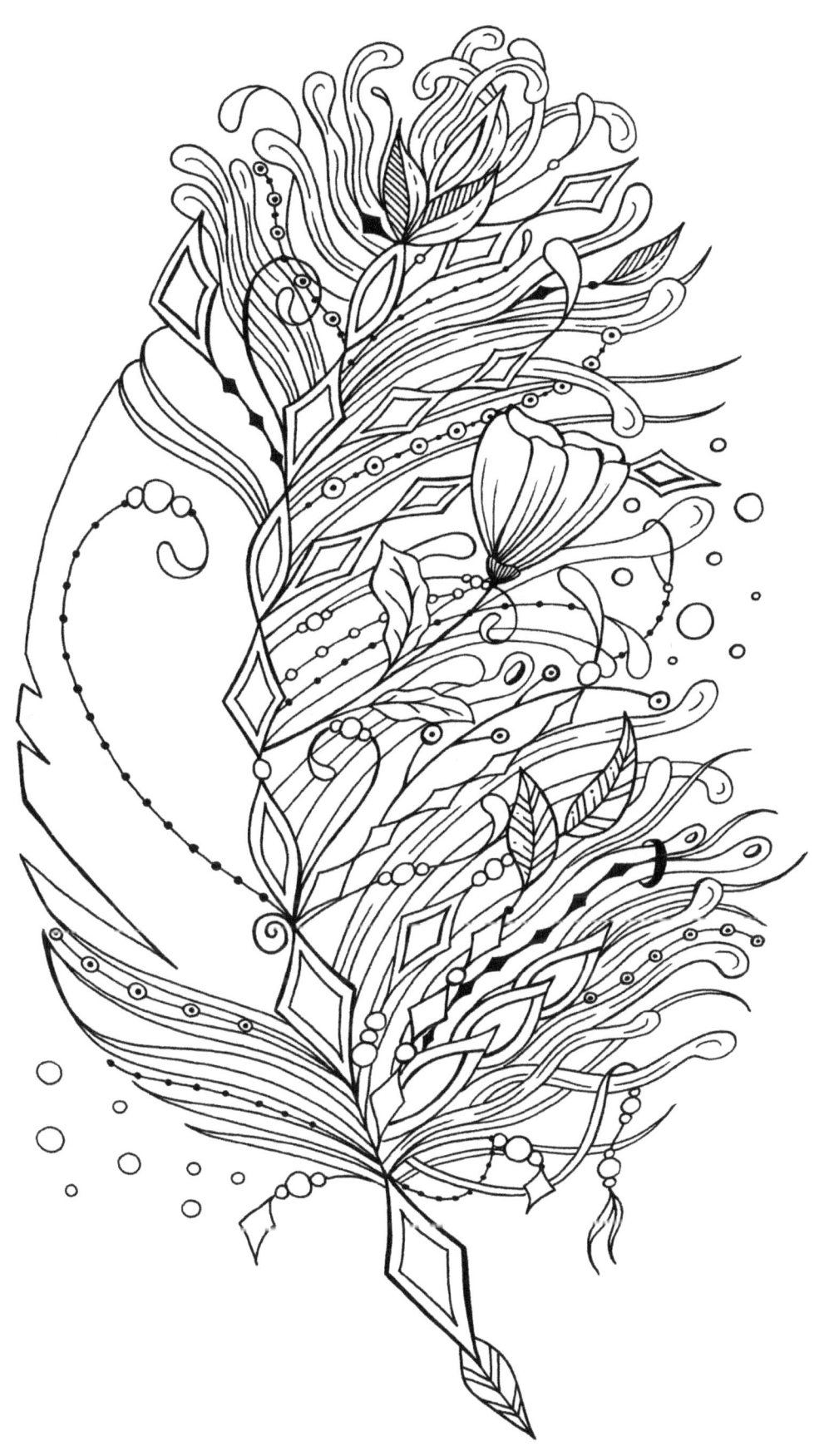

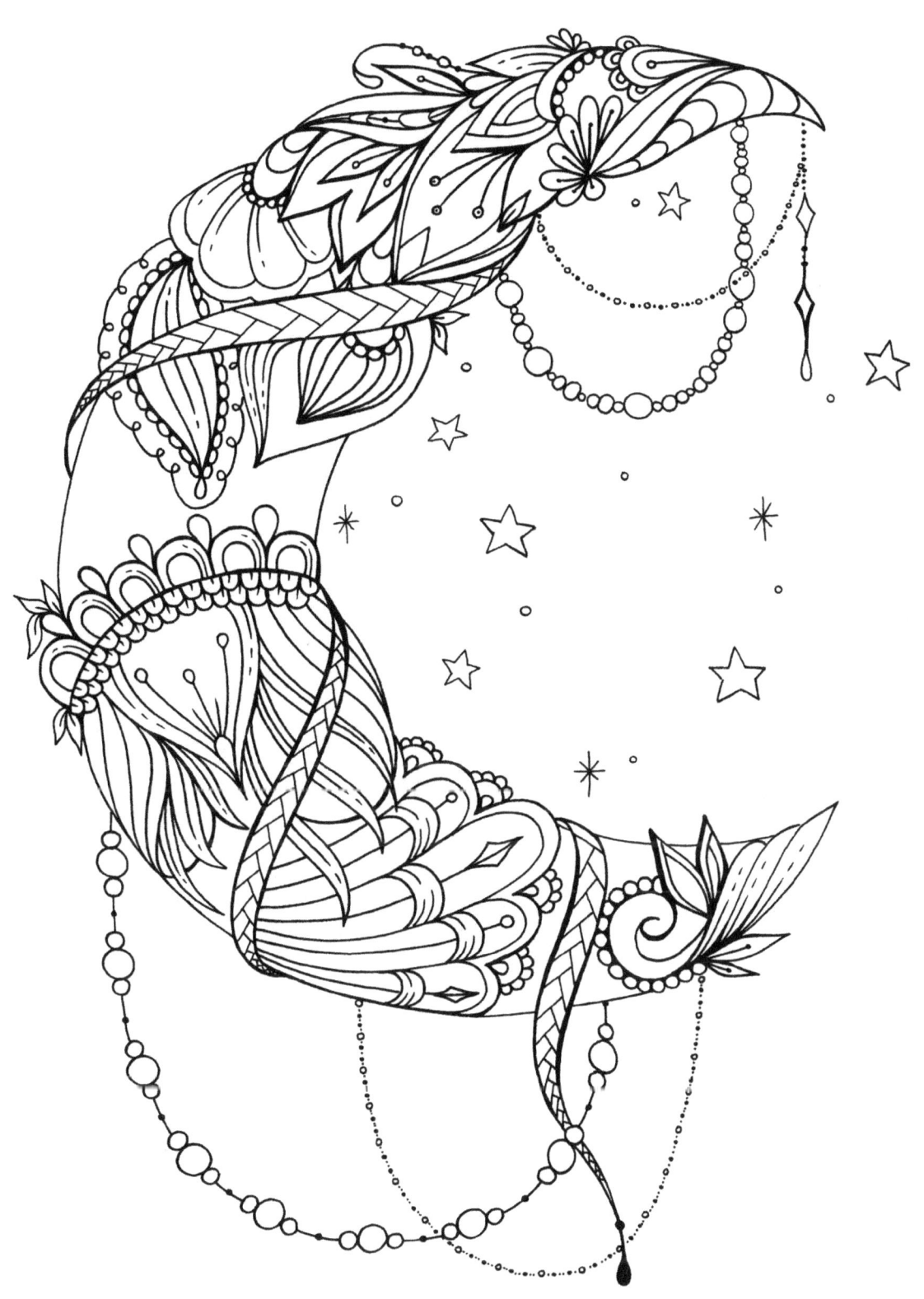

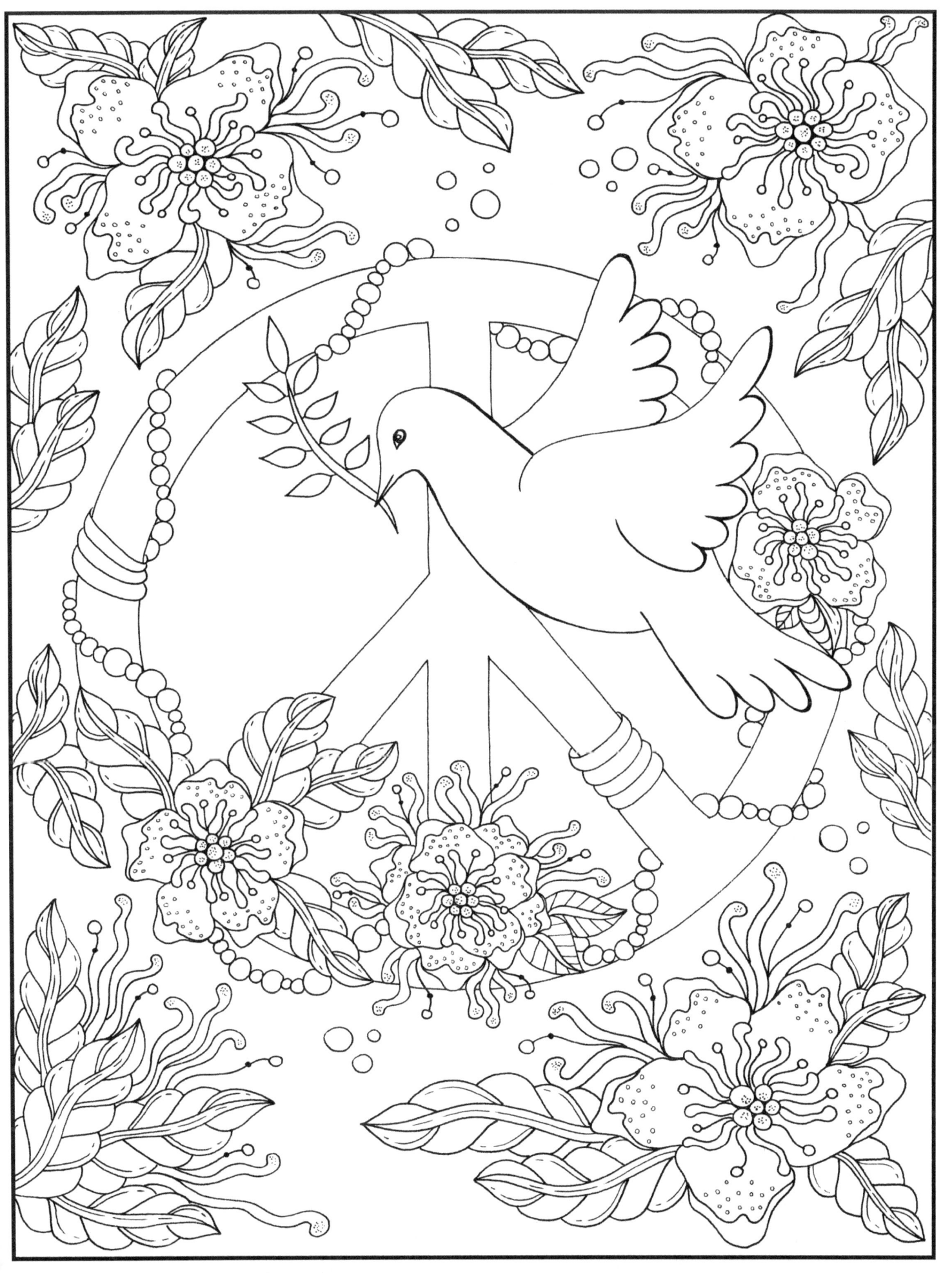

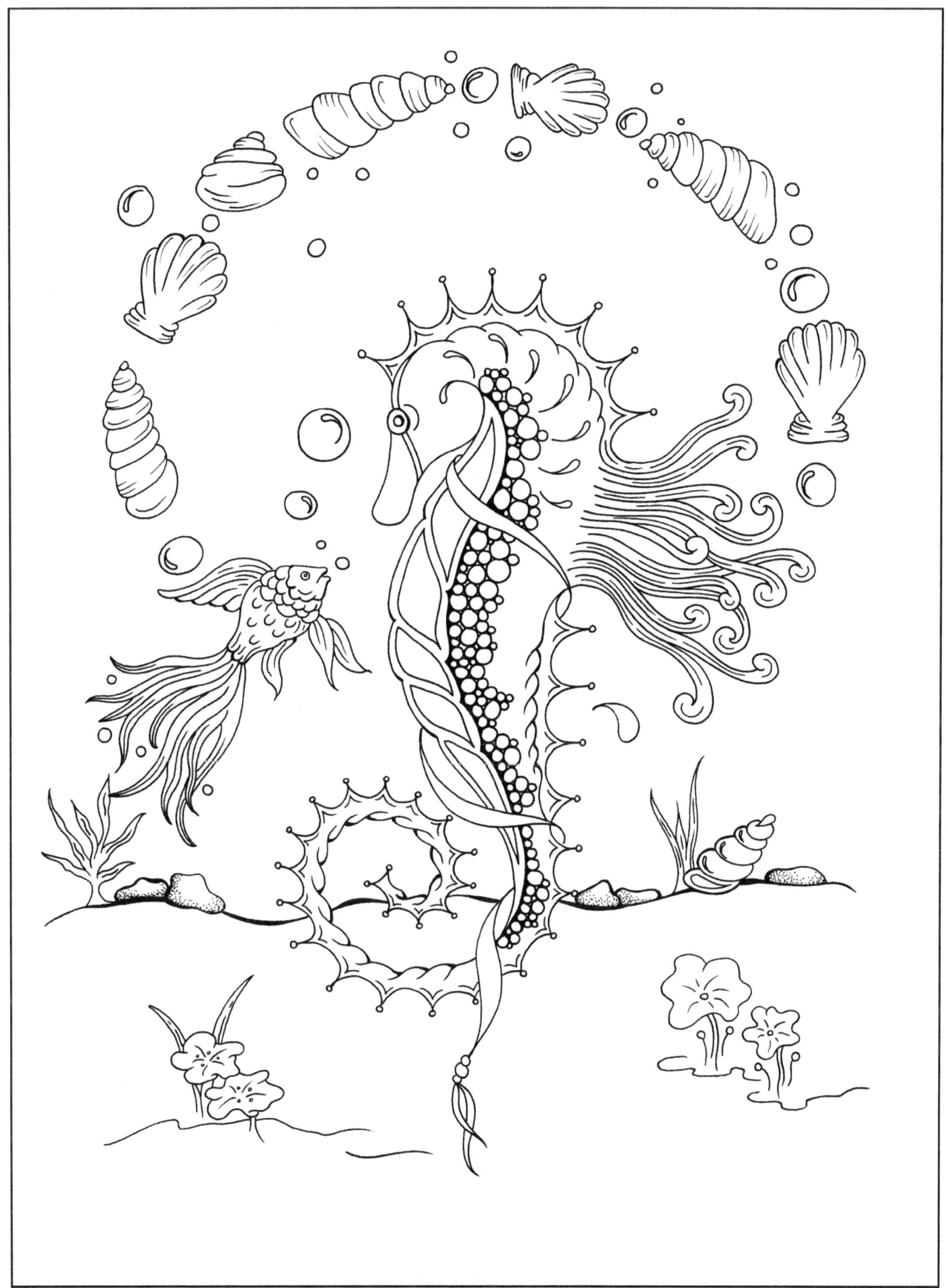

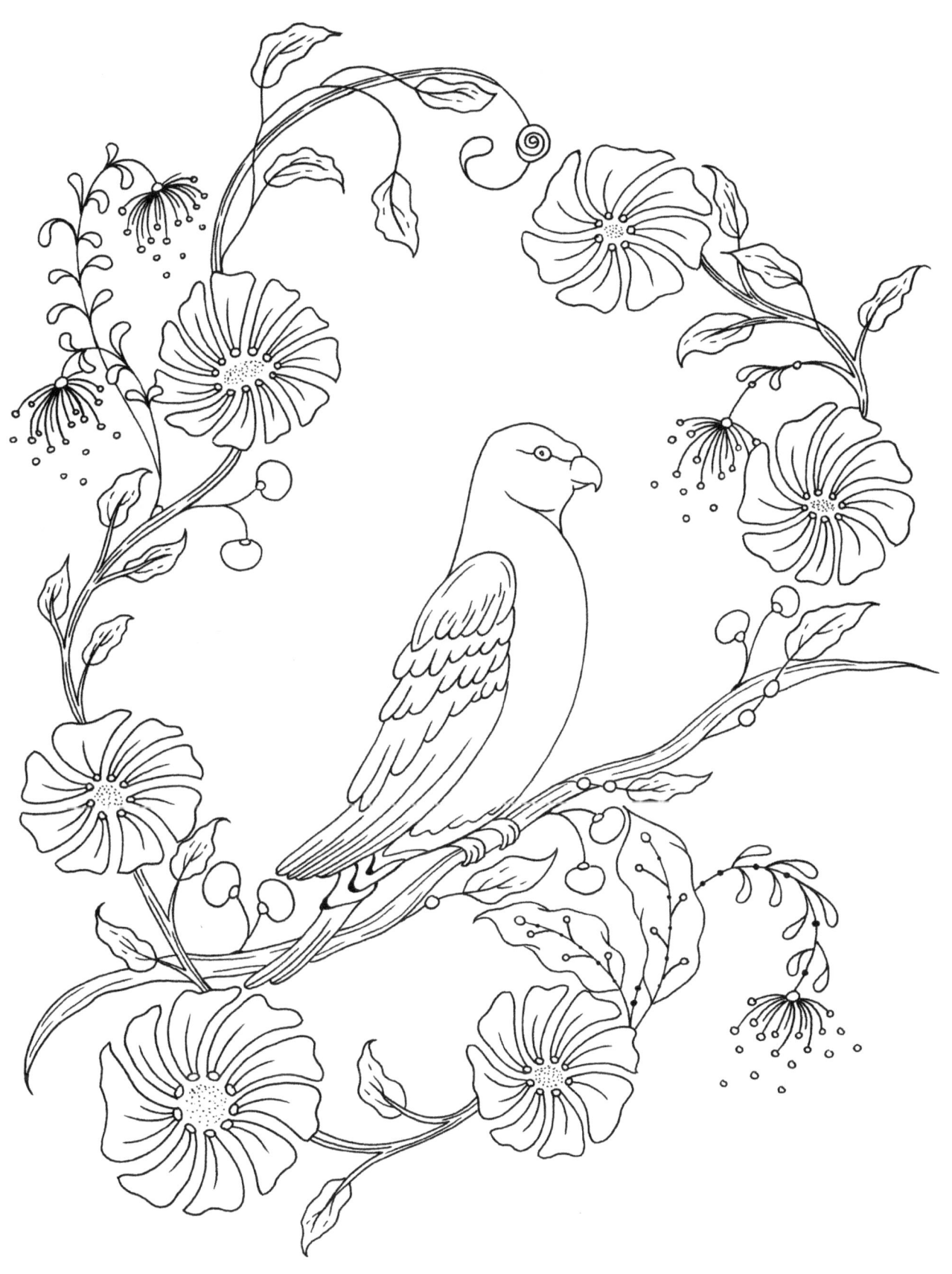

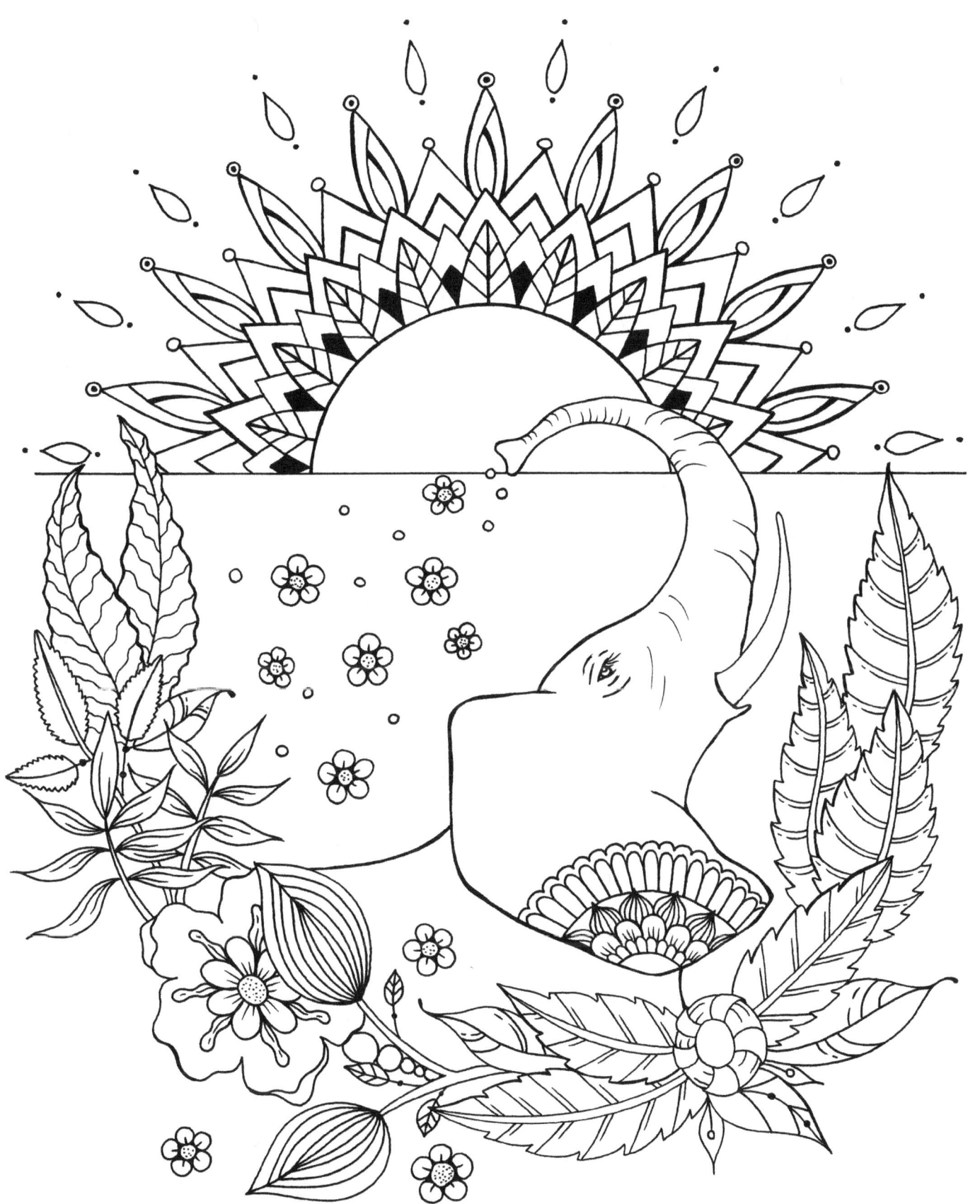

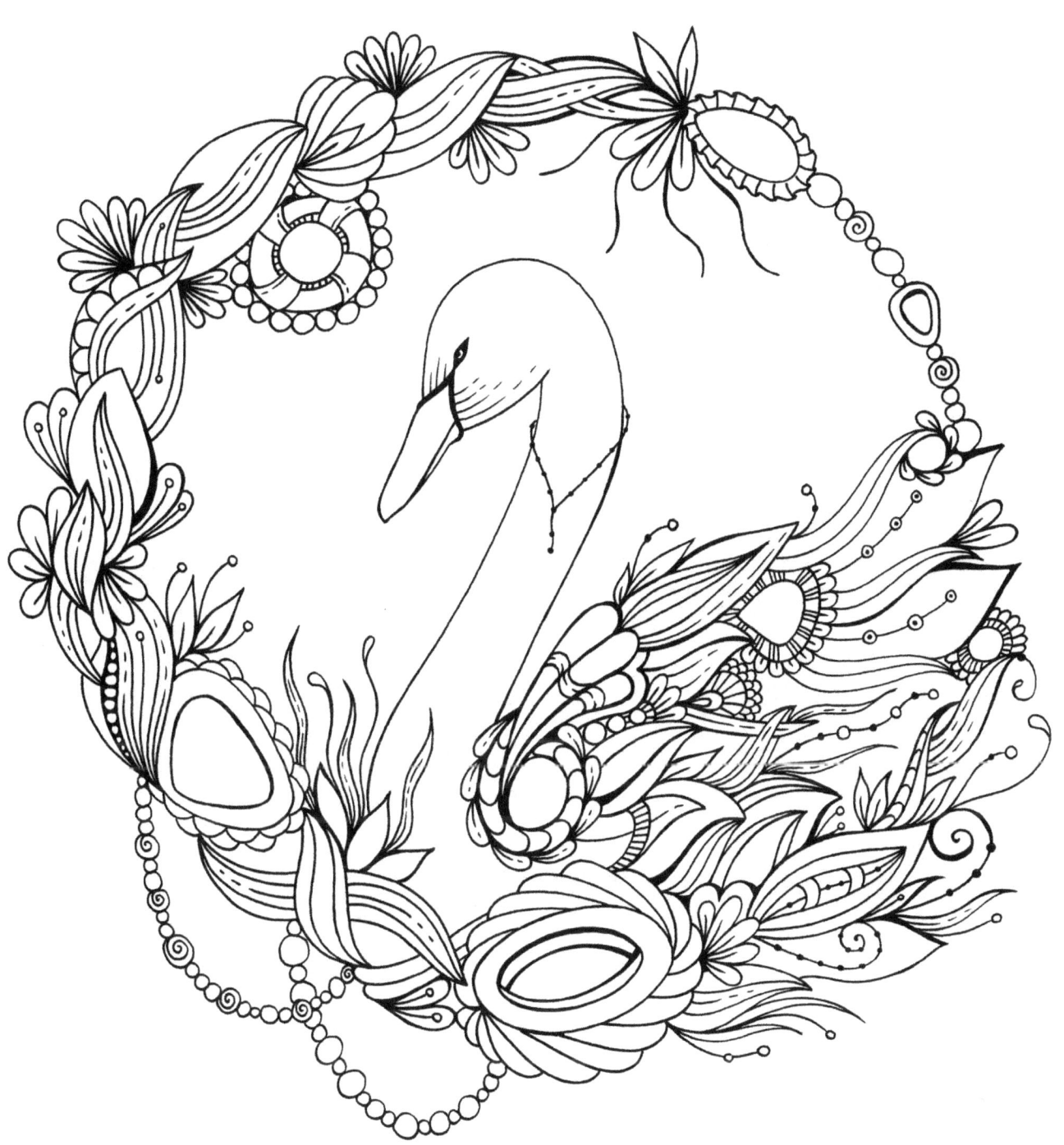

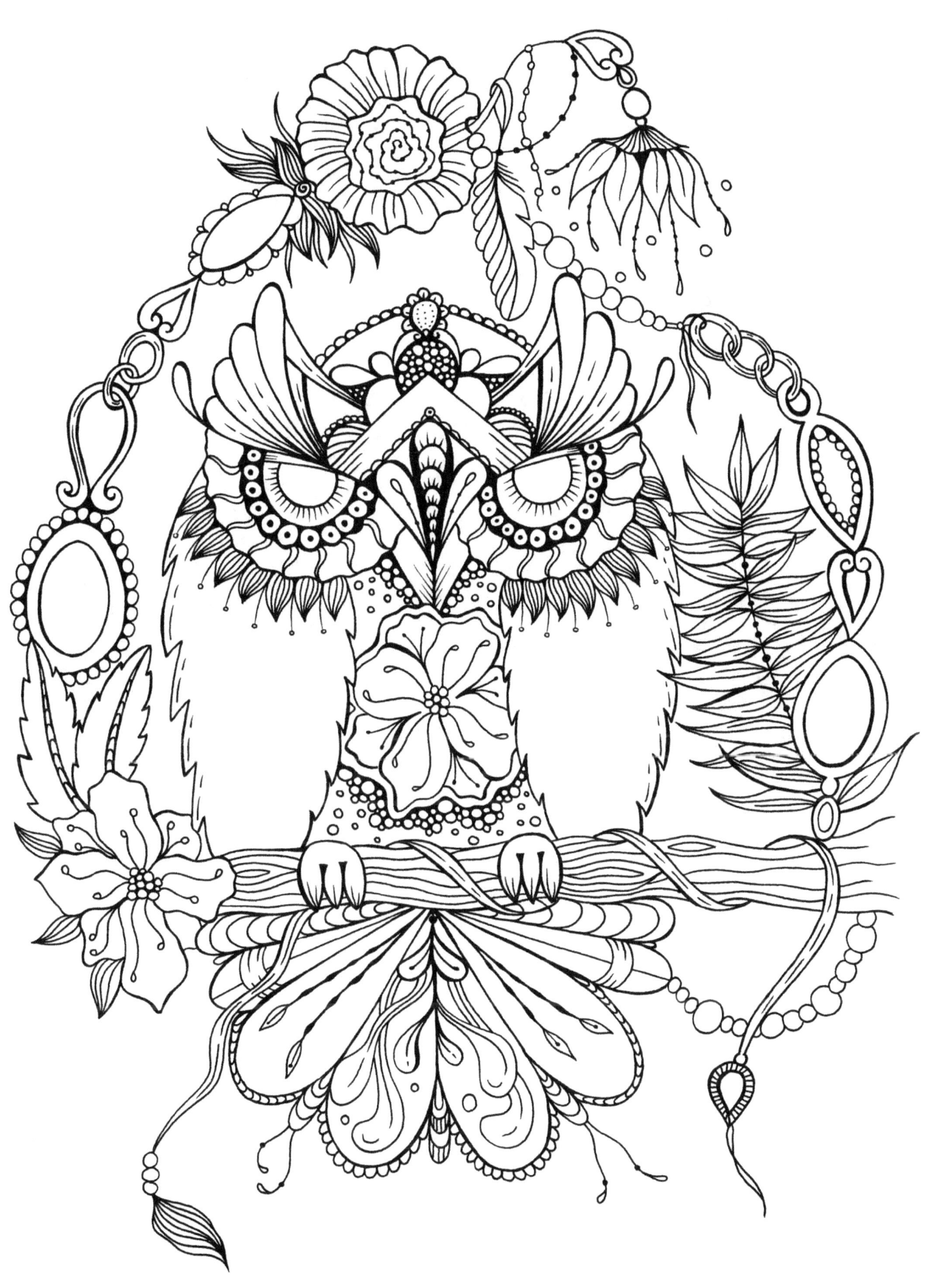

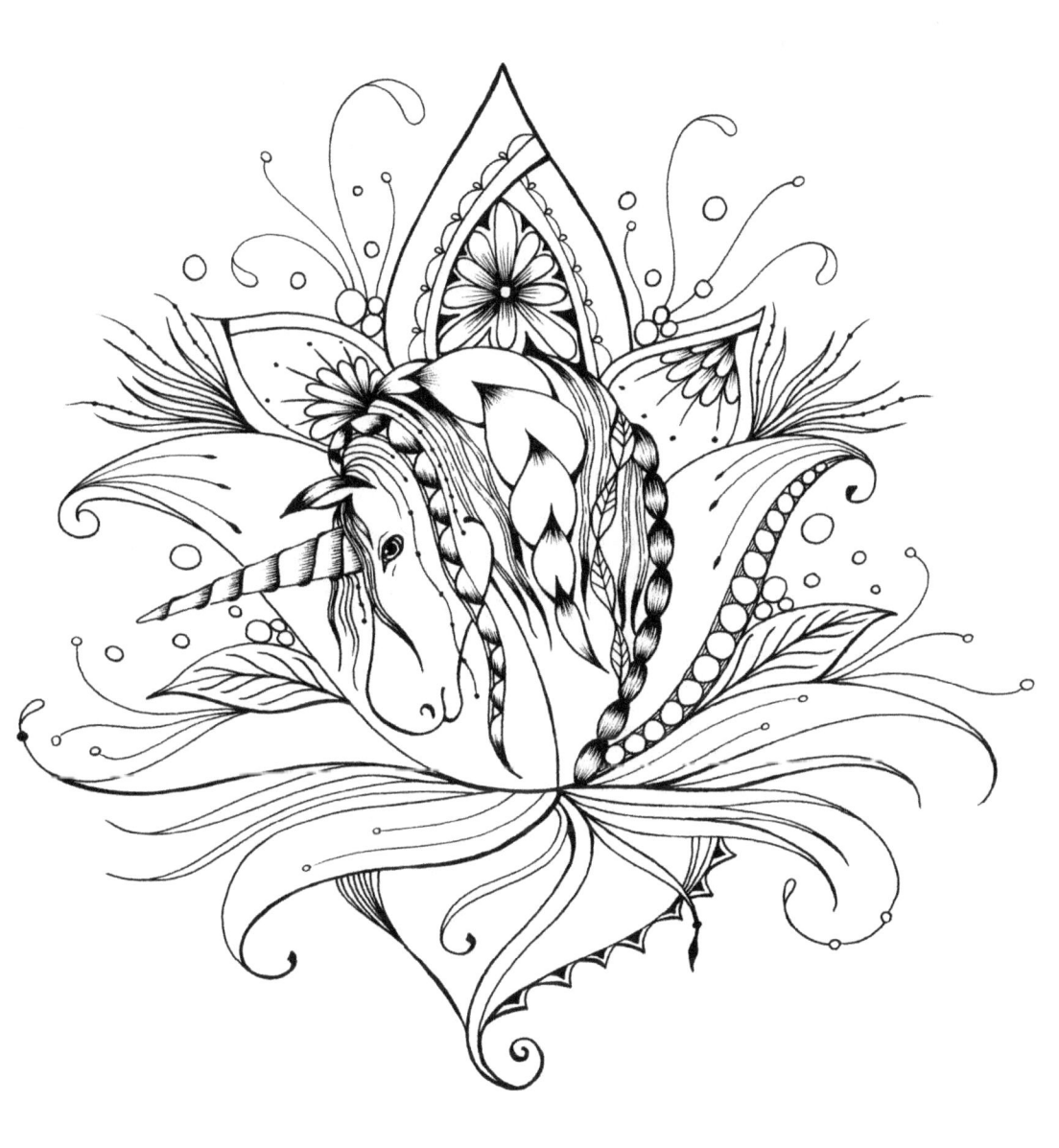

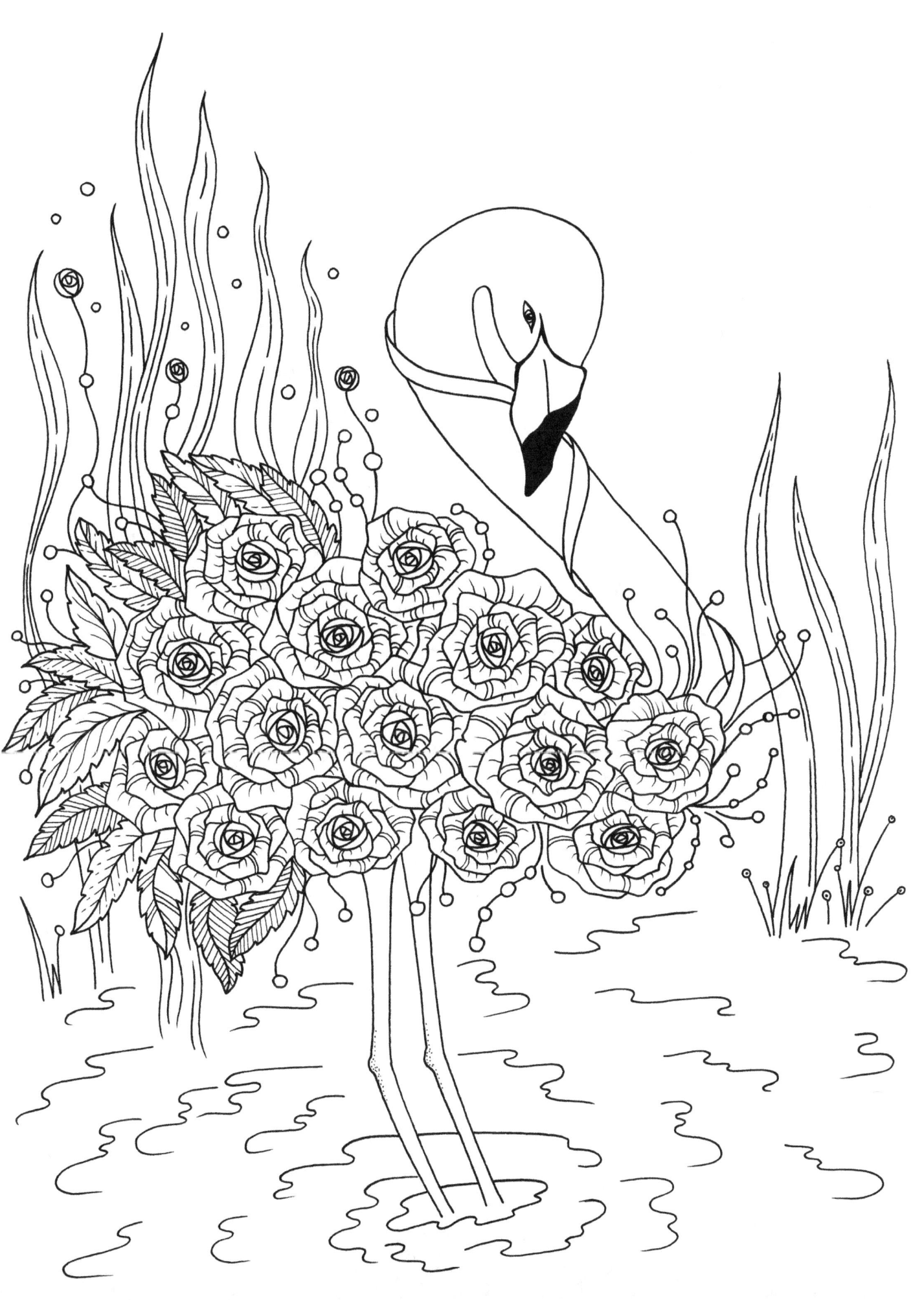

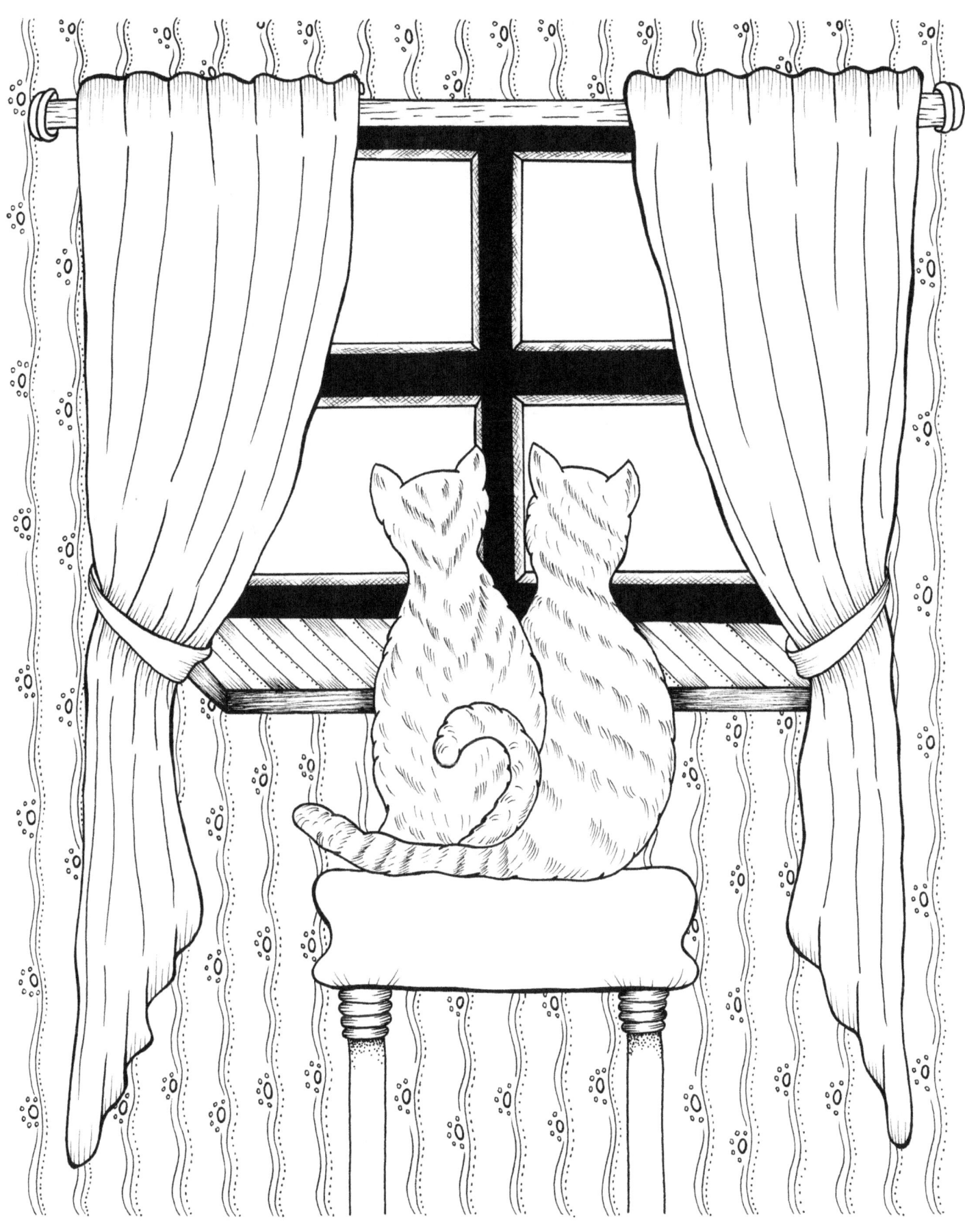

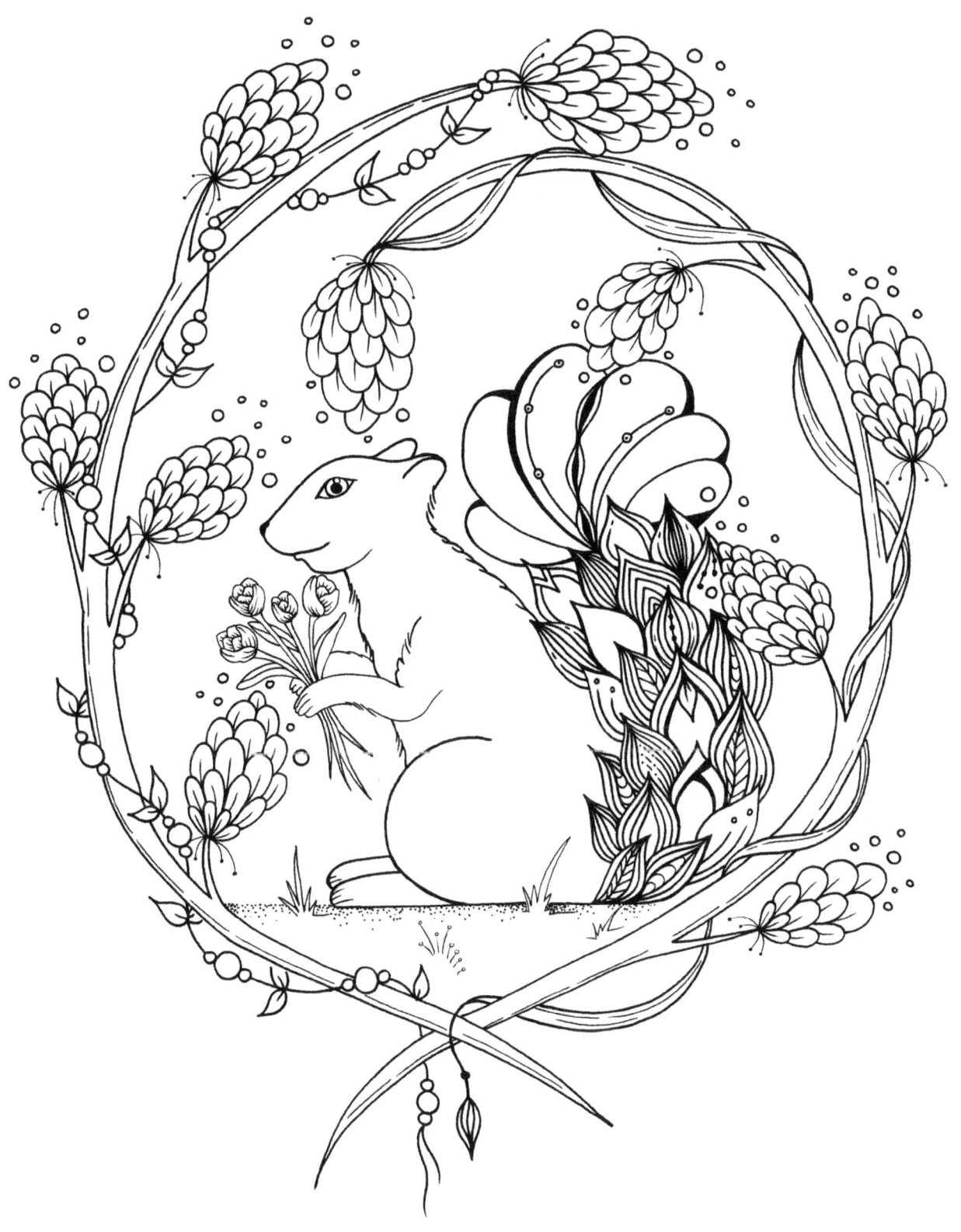

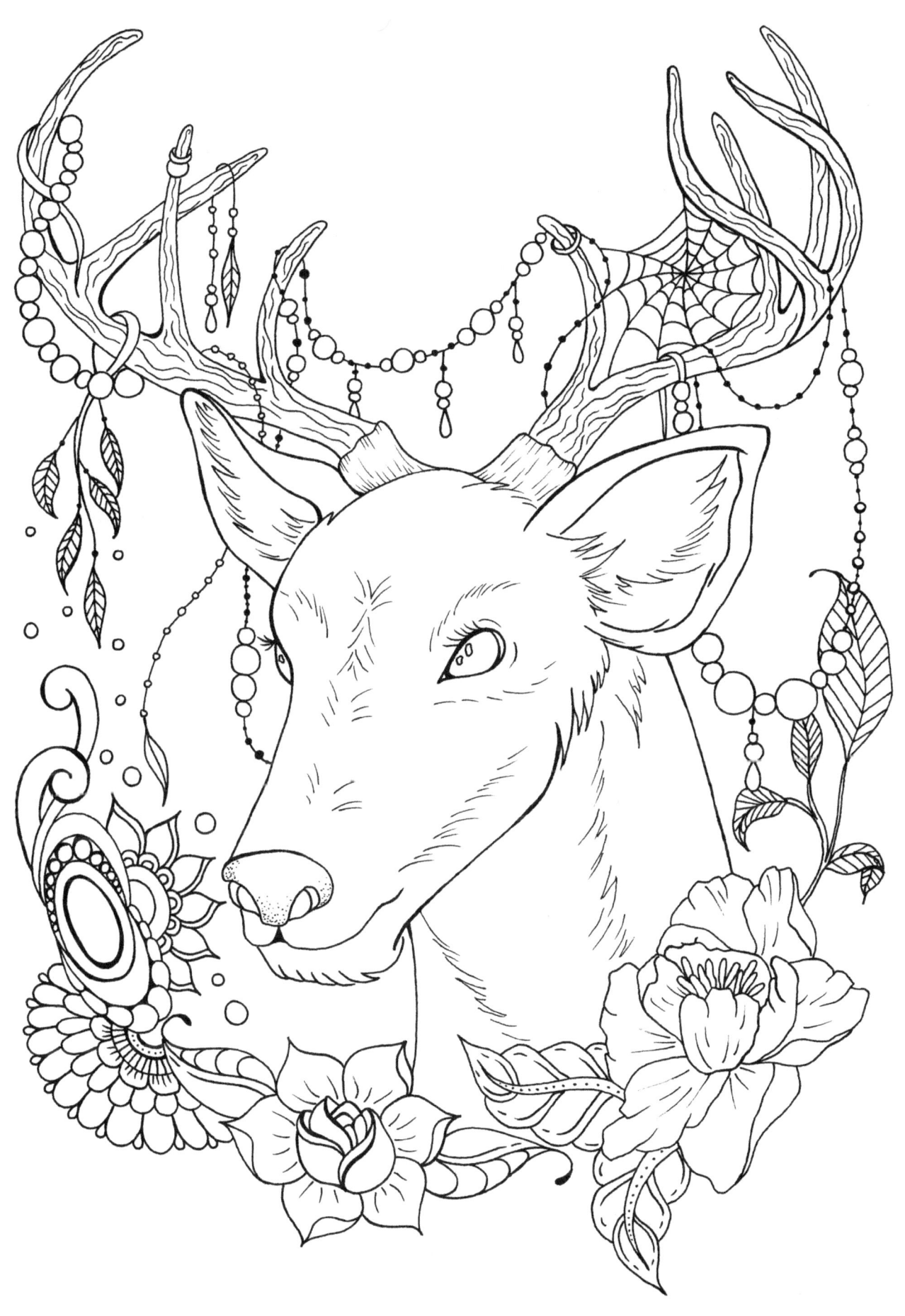

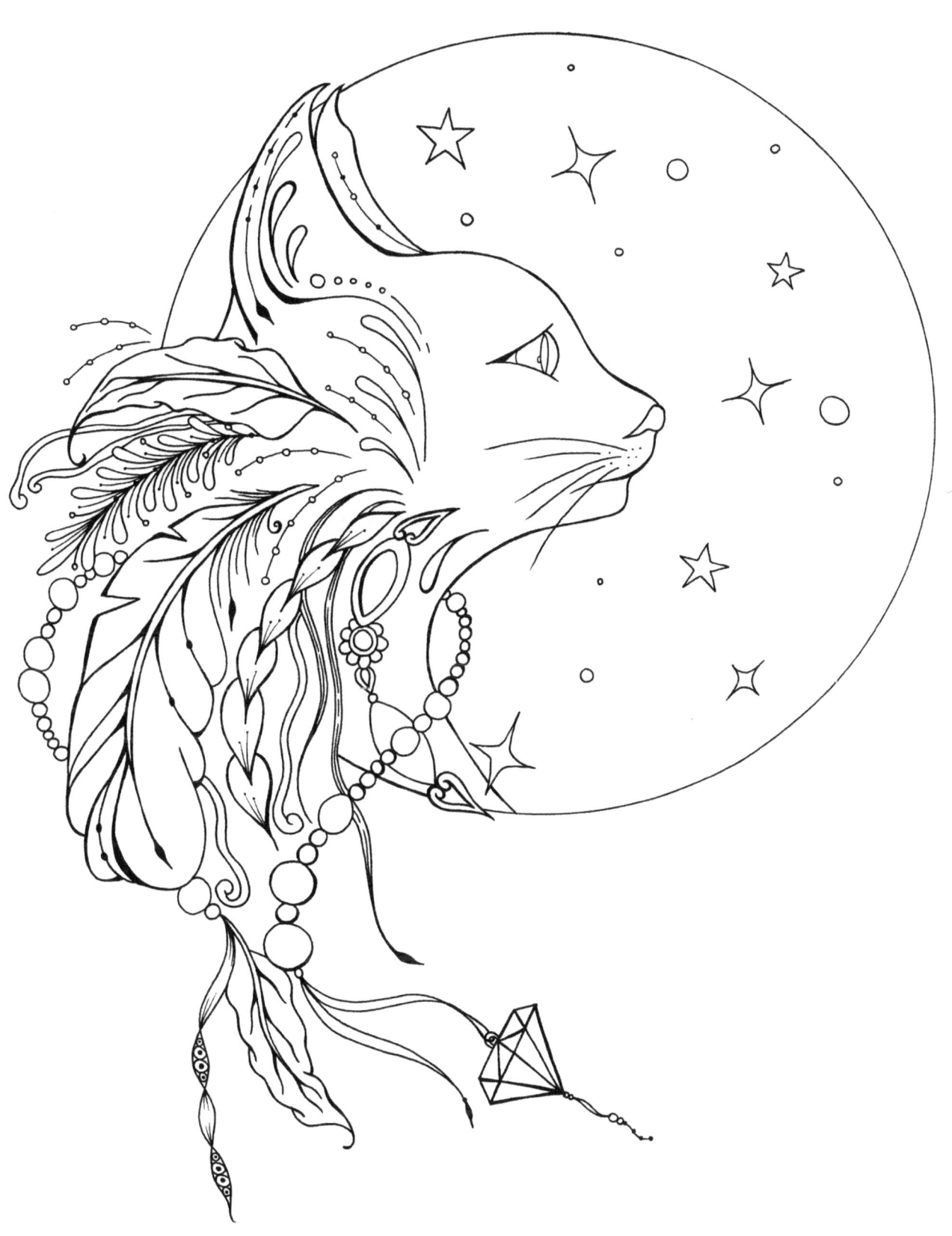

www.ingramcontent.com/pod-product-compliance
Lightning Source LLC
Chambersburg PA
CBHW062156220526
45470CB00009B/2842